VOTING IN REVOLUTIONARY AMERICA

★★★★★★★★★★★★★★

Recent titles in
Contributions in American History

VOTING IN REVOLUTIONARY AMERICA

★★★★★★★★★★★★★★

A Study of Elections in the Original Thirteen States, 1776-1789

Robert J. Dinkin

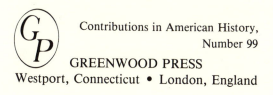

Contributions in American History,
Number 99

GREENWOOD PRESS
Westport, Connecticut • London, England

Library of Congress Cataloging in Publication Data

Dinkin, Robert J.
  Voting in revolutionary America.

  (Contributions in American history, ISSN 0084-9219 ;
no. 99)
  Continues: Voting in provincial America.
  Bibliography: p.
  Includes index.
  1. Elections—United States—History. 2. United
States—Politics and government—Revolution, 1775–1783.
3. United States—Politics and government—1783–1789.
I. Title. II. Series.
JK1965.D54   324.973'02   81-13266
ISBN 0-313-23091-9 (lib. bdg.)   AACR2

Library of Congress Catalog Card Number: 81-13266
ISBN: 0-313-23091-9
ISSN: 0084-9219

First published in 1982

Greenwood Press
A division of Congressional Information Service, Inc.
88 Post Road West, Westport, Connecticut 06881

Printed in the United States of America

10 9 8 7 6 5 4 3 2 1

Contents

Tables

Preface

The volume is intended to be a sequel to my previous work, *Voting in Provincial America: A Study of Elections in the Thirteen Colonies, 1689–1776* (Westport, Connecticut, 1977). I have attempted to carry forward the development of the voting process in the original thirteen states from the moment of independence to the beginning of the new government under President Washington. The subject of voting in this era has been rather neglected by historians, who have seen the 1790s, when national parties emerged, as the period of major transformation. Yet, as I try to demonstrate in these pages, most aspects of the system underwent greater change in the 1770s and 1780s. Indeed, many of the practices which we associate with modern voting started to take shape in these years.

The book is concerned primarily with popular elections on the state level—contests for seats in the various legislatures and, in the five states where it was permitted, for the governorship. Although they are not treated separately or exhaustively, the first two nationwide races—the choosing of delegates to the constitutional ratifying conventions in 1787–88 and the designation of congressmen and presidential Electors in 1788–89—are dealt with to some degree. However, since the actual selection of the first president and vice-president was made by the electoral college and did not involve public voting that phase is not included here. Neither is there much mention of local elections as data for such contests are extremely limited.

As in the earlier book, I have drawn upon a wide range of secondary materials plus many new primary materials in seeking to provide the first comprehensive analysis of the subject. Again, I treat each part of the process individually, discussing in separate chapters the general nature of the era's elections, the franchise, the candidates, nominations, electioneering, polling procedures, turnout, and voting behavior. I have focused more heavily on the newer aspects of the system in order to avoid too much repetition. Where certain practices remained unchanged in this period, the description is often quite brief. Readers desiring a fuller account of these topics are directed to the earlier volume.

I hope that this study will contribute to a clearer understanding of the origins of the nation's voting process, and how it evolved in the dozen years or so after separation from the mother country. Surely, one of the great legacies of the American Revolution was the movement toward government by the people, something that became possible only with the expanded use of the vote.

In the process of completing this work I would like to express my gratitude to the many librarians and curators of manuscript collections in the original thirteen states, especially those at the New York Historical Society, the Massachusetts Archives, the New Hampshire State Library, the Rhode Island Historical Society, and the Maryland Hall of Records. I would also like to thank the members of the reference department at the library of California State University, Fresno, for answering my many questions and enabling me to locate important materials, and former director of the library, Dr. Henry Madden, for his efforts in building up the institution's resources for historical research. Dorothy Tucci, Bertha Epperson, and Diane Rivera-Pasillas each carefully typed several chapters of the manuscript. Professor Edward M. Cook of the University of Chicago provided me with a great deal of data and also read the entire volume, saving me from a number of errors. Finally, I wish to thank my friend Dorothy Wightman, who has been very helpful to me during the last stages of the book's production and in many other ways as well.

VOTING IN REVOLUTIONARY AMERICA

★★★★★★★★★★★★★★

1

Revolutionary Era Elections

★★★★★★★★★★★★★★

The American election system underwent major change during the Revolutionary era, advancing rapidly in a modern, democratic direction. The new political forces at work profoundly altered many of the basic practices used and attitudes held prior to 1776. Elections in the provincial period had generally been carried on in a low-key manner, dominated by the gentleman class and characterized by much indifference. With a few notable exceptions voter turnout had not been very high. Legal restrictions under the crown, inaccessibility of polling sites, lack of formal parties and ongoing issues, and a feeling of deference toward the elite, had circumscribed both interest and participation.[1] Following independence, these conditions started to fade, opening the door to large-scale transformation. To be sure, reform did not touch every aspect; some traditional forms and methods were retained and would persist for a long time afterward. Yet the main thrust of activity was clearly forward, and an electoral process with many new modes soon came into being.

The new and more modern election system was the product of numerous developments. Perhaps the most significant was the demise of British rule. After separation from the mother country, practically all royal and proprietary influence disappeared from American politics. British-appointed governors fell from power. Factions which had supported the crown ended up severely weakened or totally destroyed. Restrictive acts from colonial times were in many cases abandoned, and legislation passed in the New World no longer had to be approved in England. The removal of royal authority also lessened the amount of arbitrary interference at the polls. In the past, sheriffs and other officials in the colonies had often interfered with the voting process, stifling the popular will. But the new state governments, operating under carefully written constitutions and better enforced election laws, eliminated most such abuses.[2]

Many of the progressive innovations made in the conduct of elections stemmed from the ideology of the Revolution. Political leaders in America, deeply influenced by English libertarian thinkers, had come to believe that governmental power was derived from the people and that the will of the people ought to be felt in the decision-making process. Only a popularly-based government, they said, would be "equitable and adapted to the good of mankind." These men also thought that all government should be limited, exercising only that authority directly assigned to it. Otherwise, like the king and Parliament in England, acting with almost no restraints, rulers here might become oppressive. Thus, they sought to create safeguards which would give the ordinary citizen greater control and compel the officials in charge to remain accountable to him. Although most framers of the new constitutions and subsequent statutes had no desire to bring about complete democracy, their efforts moved the thirteen states a considerable degree in that direction.[3]

To accelerate the growth of popular control every state made more of its governmental posts elective instead of appointive. During the provincial years, usually just the lower house of the legislatures and some local positions were elective. Now, the upper houses and, in several cases, governors and other administrative officers were popularly chosen. In addition, the framers everywhere curtailed the power of the new senate and chief executive, the latter generally being denied use of the veto. Meanwhile, the assembly, the people's branch, gained further ascendancy, especially in regard to financial matters. Other structural alterations directly connected with the election system included less stringent requirements for voting and officeholding, expanded and more equitable representation, regular and frequent contests, greater use of the paper ballot, and increased numbers of polling places. All these modifications afforded many Americans the opportunity to play a bigger role in the political life of the new nation.

But perhaps as important as institutional reform was the growing politicization of the common man. Formerly apathetic, a large segment of the population found itself increasingly drawn into the political realm by the stirring events of the Revolutionary epoch. Thousands of colonists began taking part in various kinds of protest activities, such as boycotts and local meetings, to voice their disapproval of British measures. "The mob begin to think and to reason," observed Gouverneur Morris of New York. The people's entry onto the public stage was hastened by the wider dissemination of news and the efforts of propagandists such as Thomas Paine, who, as Jack P. Greene has recently shown, "was the herald of the linear rationality of the emerging typographically literate society." Paine and other writers gave the typical American an appreciation of his own social virtue and inner worth, and made him see the need to become politically active.[4]

For many colonials, political awakening came about through direct participation in the war effort. From their personal involvement they became openly and actively committed to the American cause. Some served on local committees of correspondence or committees of safety, others joined the state militia or the Continental army. In all of these organizations individuals quickly grew aware of what was happening around them and became more conscious of their political rights. Moreover, once having occupied positions of prominence, men from the lower ranks felt reluctant to resume a subordinate role. As John Eliot of Boston told Reverend Jeremy Belknap in early 1777: "It is a rare thing to meet anybody here without some lofty titles to declare their merit—Colonel A., Major B., Captain C., denominates every puppy that 'bays the moon'. Of the very small part who are undistinguished by military habiliments, you can find none who do not think themselves *somehow* above their neighbors. To suppose a person is a mechanic is an affront."[5]

The new posture exhibited by the people began to undermine the traditional politics of deference. The average citizen who in the previous era passively accepted rule by the rich and well-born was no longer willing to do so. A considerable percentage of the upper class had taken the Tory side and even wealthy Patriots could not always be trusted, particularly after incidents of corruption were made known. Many "common men" now saw the need to act and to speak out themselves on crucial matters. "Every drabbling dishclout politician, however various their opinions, have all some kind of observation to make upon the times," insisted one contemporary.[6] When election day neared, "the curiosity and interest of the inhabitants were aroused," remarked another.[7] Public apathy was giving way to growing concern. Nevertheless, the world was not turned completely upside down. An astute foreign visitor, Count Francesco dal Verme of Milan, after watching the assembly contest in Philadelphia in 1783, noted that despite the wider range of participants, "the rich," in this country as elsewhere, were "more influential than others."[8] Yet, on the whole, men of affluence did not dominate the election scene to the extent they had before independence.

As deferential politics declined, the overall function of voting started to expand. Until this time, the voter's role had by custom been limited to choosing the best man among rival candidates without any thought of influencing him in regard to future policy or legislation. But during the Revolutionary era many people came to the conclusion that their representative, instead of being a free agent, should be made to reflect the views of those electing him. This caused a tremendous rise in the number of communities instructing their legislators on what position to take on vital questions. "From the nature of a government by representation, the deputies must be subject to the wills of their principals," declared Samuel Chase, a popular leader in Maryland during the Confederation.[9] Furthermore, the electorate was now more apt to look for persons in advance who would best carry out their wishes. Thus, elections increasingly involved the promotion of constituent interests, and not merely the choice of individuals. By the late 1780s, candidates in many locales had difficulty gaining voter support without first making firm commitments on certain matters.

With voters seeking to influence public policy, elections tended to be much more issue-oriented. This offered a sharp contrast to the provincial period when most contests were decided on the basis of *who* rather than *what*. Many earlier clashes at the polls had been caused by family feuds or short-term factional disputes, that is, minor struggles for power and place. Issues in the past had generally been local, temporary, and not overly consequential. Now they were becoming national, ongoing, and extremely significant. Issues connected with wartime problems or the postwar readjustment, such as regulation of prices, paper currency, treatment of Loyalists, western lands, prewar British debts, and the impost, created widespread public concern and deeply affected the outcome of numerous state races. "Paper money or not seems to agitate the generality of the counties," reported Edmund Randolph shortly before a Virginia election.[10] Similar words were frequently echoed elsewhere.

Divisions arising from these issues eventually led to the growth of new political factions which were more organized, stable, and far-reaching than earlier groupings. As Jackson T. Main has demonstrated, two relatively continuous and cohesive legislative parties appeared sooner or later in almost every state during the Revolutionary era. Most historians have referred to the competing sides as "Conservatives" and "Radicals" but, as Main says, they might more accurately be called "Commercial-Cosmopolitans" and "Agrarian-Localists." The first comprised chiefly business and professional men who resided in or near urban settings. Sometimes they allied themselves with large landowners who had similar economic interests. Many of these individuals were well educated, had considerable worldly experience, and possessed a broad or "continental" outlook. In contrast, their Localist adversaries were usually small farmers who produced relatively little for distant markets. The latter lived mostly in isolated rural areas far from trade and cultural centers. Unlike the Cosmopolitans, they often lacked formal education and worldly experience, and displayed a narrow or provincial outlook.

As far as issues were concerned, the Commercial-Cosmopolitans, being wealthier, tended to more willingly accept taxation and government spending, but wanted a hard and stable currency. They generally showed greater sympathy for Loyalists and criticized confiscation of their property. The Cosmopolitans also came to favor a stronger central government. On the other hand, the Agrarian-Localists, spokesmen for the less affluent, opposed most new spending and taxation laws, and wanted no change in the form of government. While neither group had the permanence and clear identity of later parties, both operated in much the same fashion. The two sides, Main points out, normally voted along strictly partisan lines, and subsequently began contending with each other at the ballot box, using differences on issues as the prime focus for their appeal.[11]

As elections came to be based more and more upon issues and factional controversies, they assumed much greater political importance, strongly affecting state and national policy. For instance,

Edmund Randolph told James Madison in 1783 that if the April elections returned enough "sound Whigs" to the assembly, they would reverse the "fatal repeal" of Virginia's ratification of the proposed impost amendment.[12] The ultimate example of local contests having broader implications was provided by the struggle over the Constitution (1787–88). The American voter influenced the whole future direction of our nation's government, choosing partisan delegates (Cosmopolitans and Localists now becoming Federalists and Antifederalists) to the state ratifying conventions to decide for or against acceptance of the new document.

Of course, issues and factional conflicts did not lie at the basis of all elections. In parts of the South, personality clashes and local matters continued to be the main sources of competition for most of the era. Heated contests for sheriff in Maryland or those for house seats in Virginia before 1787 did not reflect Cosmopolitan-Localist divisions. Disagreement among factions, however strong, was principally confined to meetings of the legislature. Even in New England and the Middle States personal and family rivalries dominated many races. The battles between John Sullivan and John Langdon for the governorship of New Hampshire, for instance, probably had more to do with the characters of the two individuals than with the public positions they espoused. Yet it is clear that even these encounters were more issue-related than the ones involving Samuel Ward and Stephen Hopkins in provincial Rhode Island twenty years earlier.[13]

Competitive elections of any kind were not too common at the beginning of the Revolutionary period. Outside of Pennsylvania and Delaware, little or no struggle occurred at the polls before the 1780s. Wartime dislocations, the presence of the British army, and the large degree of Whig unity reduced the possibilities for heated encounters. In some areas it was fortunate that balloting could be held at all considering the circumstances. But once peace was established, the number of genuine contests picked up precipitously. In 1785, Archibald Stuart of Virginia claimed that "Competition for seats in the house run higher than ever they Did under the Old government."[14] Over the next two years, economic and political problems, which culminated in the calling of the Constitutional Convention, stimulated partisan activity even further. By the time of the ratification process (1787–88) and the choice of members to the first Congress (1788–89), rival groups in almost every state had begun to organize slates of candidates and to campaign vigorously for office.[15]

While overall competition was on the rise, the amount of it clearly varied from region to region and state to state, as the following survey of elections from 1776 to 1789 indicates. As in the provincial period, the southern states, especially those of the lower South—the Carolinas and Georgia—experienced the smallest number of hard-fought elections. The predominantly rural environment and the greater homogeneity of those within the political community made for much less strife than elsewhere. The debates over the issues that at times emerged were generally limited to the legislative sessions. Except in a very few places (mostly urban locales), factional discord did not lead to many contests at the polls until the late 1780s, and even then the intensity of the campaigns did not match that of the ones further north.

Georgia, the last of the thirteen colonies to be founded and the least developed politically, continued to have few competitive elections in this era. In fact, during the war years elections sometimes could not be held at all. Regular polling occurred throughout most of the state from 1776 to 1778, but as the British controlled many areas from the winter of 1779 to the summer of 1782, voting was carried on in just a handful of counties. Even in those places it is not clear whether formal procedures were always followed. Amid the assembly contest in late 1781, when the British army remained a distinct threat, people in those districts "still in alarm" had to go to Augusta to cast their ballots.[16]

The election system returned to a fairly normal basis after 1782, but, compared to the twelve other states, competition here was minimal. Despite the emergence of distinctive sectional and economic interests, such divisions did not become manifest at the polls. As Kenneth Coleman has written: "Election campaigns, as the term is now understood, did not take place in post-Revolutionary Georgia. Ordinarily anyone desiring a public office left his name with the clerk of the assembly or a committee for transmission to assemblymen at the time of elections."[17] Frequently, he added, an individual who was put forth as a candidate later refused to serve. The absence of any rivalry was evident even in the designation of members to the constitutional ratifying convention. Although no absolute unanimity prevailed, few districts offered alternative slates and only a minor amount of electioneering was undertaken. Because of the Indian menace and other problems, the vast majority of Georgians saw the need for a stronger central government. At least two-thirds of the delegates chosen were pro-Federal, and the rest soon converted. The next year (1788), in the choice of representatives to the first federal Congress, no major conflict developed and the voters elected Federalists in all three cases.[18]

South Carolina's elections, like Georgia's, usually involved little competition or strenuous campaigning. The early state races were dominated by wealthy Cosmopolitan families such as the Pinckneys, the Rutledges, the Middletons, and the Laurenses. Then British occupation prevented any voting at all in the early 1780s. But even after the process was restored in 1783, the record reveals few bona fide contests. Although backcountry residents had a number of grievances against the powerful easterners running the legislature, especially for their unwillingness to grant adequate representation, this animosity did not have any reverberations at the polls. Most candidates ran unopposed and voter turnout was invariably small. The story told in the provincial period about the church wardens being the only persons in some parishes to cast ballots may still have applied on certain occasions.[19]

One major exception to this chronic indifference occurred in the election of 1784, most notably in the city of Charleston. The planter and professional elite, who had long monopolized the government, came under sharp attack from the less well-to-do, who were led by the self-made merchant Alexander Gillon. "The Malcontented party," it was said, had in "several publications endeavoured to influence the Electors throughout the State to make choice of Men to represent them in the General Assembly, from the lower class." Gillon's forces accused their opponents (popularly known as Nabobs) of being pro-Tory and against the poor; they in turn were characterized by Cosmopolitan publicists as "Drunken Tavern-keepers, Montebank Doctors, Pettifogging Attornies and Necessitous Speculators." The latter charges must have carried more weight, for in the balloting the so-called "democratical party" was defeated by a large margin.[20] According to John Lloyd, a Charleston merchant, "The gentlemen of property, to preserve their necessary consequence in the community and in order to prevent anarchy and confusion, have almost unanimously exerted themselves in opposition to them, and . . . have pretty generally carried their point.''[21] The Nabobs experienced somewhat less difficulty at election time over the next several years, and maintained full control of the legislature.

The only other election in South Carolina to be contested on a fairly broad basis featured the choice of delegates to the constitutional ratifying convention in 1788. While the campaign lacked real fervor, western opposition to the Nabob leadership slowly congealed, and voting followed sectional lines. The Localist, or Antifederalist, bloc succeeded throughout most of the inland farming region, but the Nabobs, now called Federalists, won heavily in the coastal plantation areas and in the city of Charleston. Since the eastern section had much greater representation, the latter group put together an overall majority enabling it to secure ratification. A few months later, however, in the election of congressional representatives, where the districts were more equalized, the Antifederalists easily took four of the five seats. The sole Federalist to come out on top was William Loughton Smith of Charleston, who, after a bitter struggle, bested Alexander Gillon and the transplanted Pennsylvanian Doctor David Ramsay.[22]

North Carolina started the Revolutionary period without much internal conflict. The "Regulator" troubles had now ended, and the statewide elections in 1776 created little stir. Only three of the thirty-six counties produced heated encounters. "We are all harmony," declared future governor Abner Nash.[23] Yet within a relatively short time unity among the Whigs began to break down. By the early 1780s, two factions—Cosmopolitan and Localist—based largely on sectional and economic differences had appeared. The small band of Cosmopolitans consisted chiefly of lawyers, merchants, and planters from the eastern part of the state. The Localists, far superior in number, were mostly yeoman farmers who resided in the agrarian west. The two sides became bitterly divided on questions of taxation and finance, and also on the matter of the Loyalists and their property.[24]

While the factional struggle was confined mainly to the legislature before 1783, the postwar era saw a sharp rise in competition at the ballot box. In numerous places, especially in the commercial towns of Wilmington, Edenton, and New Bern, elections were extremely hard-fought and often violent. Because of strong anti-creditor and anti-Tory sentiment among the populace, leading Cosmopolitans such as William Hooper and Archibald Maclaine had to overcome great odds to remain in office. Never able to command a majority in either house, these nationalist-minded men did manage to block some of the more stringent measures put forth by their opponents and even slipped through a few of their own proposals.[25]

Some of the most severe contests took place in the summer of 1787 as the nationalist group, soon to be called Federalists, sought to increase its strength in both houses so as to provide a favorable reception for the new Constitution. Great bitterness was infused into the canvass, with tumults and assaults occurring at several points. In the Orange County race, the aristocratic Hooper got involved in a brawl and "came off second best, with his eyes blacked."[26] An even more vicious campaign developed the following March (1788), amid selection of delegates to the state ratifying convention. Public debate often descended to name-calling as leaders on each side were sharply denounced. Antifederalists even resorted to extreme scare tactics to gain favor, one minister claiming that under the proposed government the national army would soon come to "enslave the people."[27] As a result of these efforts, many well-known Federalists went down to defeat, causing the Constitution to be rejected in North Carolina at this time. Only after a second convention was called a year later, when fierce partisanship had begun to moderate, did election strife diminish and ratification become a reality.[28]

Virginia, which frequently experienced exciting contests in the provincial period, saw their numbers decline during the war years. "The freeholders," observed John Page in 1778, had sunk into a "torpid state, for so few of them attend at elections now that any man may get into either house."[29] The only counties to witness any conflict at the polls were those where alleged Tories tried to seek office. By 1783, however, heavy competition had resumed in many areas. "Contests are very warm among the [planters] for our approaching elections," reported Edmund Pendleton that spring.[30] The results showed that the Cosmopolitan faction was beginning to make inroads in the legislature against the dominant Localists led by Patrick Henry. "I think our Elections, as far as I have hitherto heard of them, have generally been in fav[o]r of the best men," Pendleton later informed James Madison.[31]

The legislature split over several momentous issues during the mid-1780s—payment of British debts, western lands, navigation of the Mississippi River, and religious liberty—though it is not clear what percentage of the electors were influenced by these questions at the polling place. In most races, the average freeholder continued to decide on the basis of men rather than measures. Yet one issue did eventually have a profound impact on numerous voters here: paper money. In 1787, debate over this matter prompted the Old Dominion's first statewide, issue-oriented campaign. Candidates in many locales were forced to take a public stand on the currency problem, and those who took an unpopular one often wound up defeated.[32]

Competition was further heightened the following year (1788) as the rival groups, now called Federalists and Antifederalists, grew deeply at odds over the new federal Constitution. The struggle for seats in the state ratifying convention stayed unusually close, since the Antifederalists could line up just as many prominent candidates as their well-known opponents. Prior to the voting, the "Antis" lashed out at the idea of "one consolidated system" and giving Congress immense taxing power. Through various means the Federalists worked hard to counteract these arguments. In the end, the supporters of a stronger national government obtained a slight majority and went on to achieve ratification. The Constitution and its consequences remained the key issues in the designation of representatives to the first Congress the next winter. Both factions again made a determined effort to gain the backing of the electorate. Yet once more the "Antis" came out second best as James Madison and his nationalist allies won seven of the ten available posts.[33]

In Maryland, despite the existence of factions in the legislature, few hard-fought elections took place before the latter part of the 1780s. To be sure, some vigorous clashes arose over the selection of delegates to frame the new state constitution (August 1776). But over the next decade contention at the polls was not very common. During the first half of the 1780s the issues dividing the Cosmopolitan and Localist blocs, such as taxation, British debts, and the disposition of Tory property, had little effect upon the voters. Most legislative candidates probably ran unopposed. The only deviations from this pattern of quiet, uncontested elections came in the triennially-held county sheriff races. A number of disputed outcomes were recorded in both 1782 and 1785, though these usually resulted from local differences and personalities rather than from statewide matters.[34]

Beginning in 1786, however, heated competition spread to a great many legislative encounters. The state's growing economic difficulties had pressed numerous citizens into the electoral battle, one focusing on paper money, which the Localists saw as a panacea. Backed primarily by small farmers, but also by a few affluent speculators like Samuel Chase, the paper-money advocates launched a powerful attack against the Cosmopolitans, who were entrenched hard-money men led by Charles Carroll of Carrollton. While they fared well in the assembly, the paper enthusiasts suffered heavy losses in the senate, eventually causing their currency bill to be rejected. The paper-money problem was largely resolved by the time of the next election (1787), yet a much more urgent matter had appeared: whether or not to ratify the new federal Constitution. The Localists, now emerging as Antifederalists, opposed unconditional ratification, calling for certain amendments; the Cosmopolitans, soon to be known as Federalists, favored the document as it existed. Though both sides waged aggressive campaigns, the original Constitution proved quite popular and its supporters were able to pick up several seats in the lower house.[35]

The choosing of delegates to the state ratifying convention the following April (1788) turned out to be the most grueling contest of the era in Maryland, as it was in many other places. The Antifederalists, through relentless electioneering, triumphed in a number of counties in and around Baltimore. Elsewhere in the state, however, they made much less of an effort, often not even entering candidates, helping the Federalists to amass a sizable majority. Although the Constitution received quick approval, factional wrangling continued to prevail. In the bitter and violent general election later that year, the Federalists lost some ground. Yet a few months afterward, in the first congressional race, they more than recovered, organizing a huge victory over their opponents. The "Antis" once again put up a strenuous fight, but the Federalists thwarted their allegedly "dark and villainous designs" and captured all of the six seats at stake.[36]

The Middle States—Pennsylvania, Delaware, New Jersey, and New York—witnessed much greater conflict at election time than did the South. The long-standing differences among various ethnic and religious groups, geographic and class-based economic interests, and the presence of numerous Loyalists in each state led soon to factional struggles in the legislature and then at the ballot box as well. Because at first the divisive elements were most pronounced in Pennsylvania and Delaware, these two states had many more hard-fought contests than did New York and New Jersey. Yet, by the end of the period, the latter states were beginning to reach parity and occasionally surpassed the former in the amount of tough competition.

Pennsylvania experienced the most competitive elections of any state during the Revolutionary era. From the very start, intense factionalism appeared not only in the legislature but at the polls as two opposing groups fervently strove for popular support. On one side were the Constitutionalists (corresponding to Localists), vigorous defenders of the state's new democratic constitution, economic reforms, and an all-out war effort. On the other side was the more cosmopolitan element, the Republicans, who condemned the lack of checks on the legislature, the new monetary policies, and the stringent "test laws" applied to neutrals and Loyalists. Although they eventually fell into disfavor, the Constitutionalists, backed by middling farmers and artisans (especially among the Presbyterians), effectively maintained themselves in power for several years, denouncing their merchant-led rivals as aristocrats and Tories.

In the first assembly elections in the fall of 1776, the Republicans won in the city and county of Philadelphia, but the Constitutionalists obtained a majority elsewhere and took charge of running the government. While the presence of the British and American armies limited the voting to a small number of counties in 1777, the Constitutionalists encountered few problems in staying on top. The Republicans struck back and made some gains in 1778, yet they still controlled only one-third of the house. Then, in 1779, they slid further behind as their opponents capitalized on the people's wrath toward the questionable business activities of the wealthy Robert Morris and James Wilson. But in 1780, when the Constitutionalists failed to stop the state's severe economic downturn, the Republicans scored significant triumphs, emerging with a majority in the assembly for the first time. The Republicans retained their high position in the following three elections (1781–83), fighting off opposition attacks and gradually implementing their own financial program.[37]

The year 1784 saw a halt in the Republican drive as the pendulum swung back toward the Constitutionalists. Hostile to a repeal of the test laws and to changes in the state constitution, the voters gave the party a victory in every county except Chester and York. This upsurge, however, did not last long; Constitutionalist excesses over the next several months led to a conservative revival in the 1785 race, the two factions then being about equal in strength. A year later, the Republicans went into the lead to stay, winning some of the hardest-fought contests of the decade as the Constitutionalists started to decline in strength. By 1787, the Republicans had assumed full command, easily capturing most house seats, and sometimes facing only token opposition.

The Republicans, or Federal Republicans, as they now called themselves, also achieved a resounding success in the designation of members to the state ratifying convention, winning a two-thirds majority. Using some questionable methods, they managed to schedule the vote early and then bombarded the populace with criticism of their adversaries, referring to them as "opportunists." The Constitutionalists, or Antifederalists, kept up their hold on some of the western counties, alarming voters with talk of aristocracy and monarchy, but they lost heavily in Philadelphia and in the eastern counties where these words had little effect. The Federal Republicans continued their upward climb in the 1788 assembly elections and in the choice of representatives to the first federal Congress. The Constitutionalists had become just a small minority by this point, but they would soon reemerge, forming the backbone of the Jeffersonian party in Pennsylvania in the 1790s.[38]

The small state of Delaware provided the scene for some of the most zealously fought and violent elections held anywhere in the Revolutionary era. An almost even split among the inhabitants into Whigs and Tories created tremendous antagonism at the polls for many years. The Whigs, cosmopolitan in outlook, were predominant in the northern section (New Castle County), which was highly Presbyterian and commercial; the Tories, or Conservatives, more localist in leaning, were strongest in the southern part (Sussex County), which was mainly Anglican and agrarian; divided Kent County was in the center, often holding the balance of power. Even after the war, the feud between the two groups continued, influencing alignments at election time throughout the 1780s.

Heated competition flared up at the very beginning as each side sought to dominate the state's delegation to the constitutional convention in August, 1776. Although the Whigs made a vigorous effort, the Conservatives were more successful, acquiring a majority of seats. The legislative elections in October, with the exception of New Castle, went no better for the Whigs. They lost in Kent County and their supporters in Sussex were prevented from voting by an armed mob of Tories, who later cut down the Liberty Pole and gave huzzahs for King George and General Howe. In 1777, however, the threat engendered by the British occupation of nearby areas led to a reversal at the ballot box. The Whigs attained victories in both New Castle and Kent, while in Sussex the militia literally chased Tory sympathizers from the polling place. When, in a new Sussex election, most Conservatives stayed away, the Whigs won there too. Over the next five years, contests became somewhat more subdued. Many among the pro-British element refused to take the oath of allegiance to qualify, allowing the Whigs complete mastery of almost every race.[39]

Yet, starting in 1783, conflict at election time quickly resumed, as former Tories could now take part. Major clashes arose in all three counties that year, the Conservatives picking up considerable strength. The Whigs regained full control of the legislature during the next two encounters—in 1784 and 1785—but in 1786, the Conservatives secured a majority in the lower house because people had grown tired of the Whig leadership. On each of these occasions, campaigning proved extremely bitter, with several altercations being reported. The climax came in 1787, when rioting by armed militia bands in Sussex County caused a great deal of bloodshed. Moreover, the results of the balloting were so sharply disputed that a second election had to be held. Irregularities marred this contest too, but the legislature, weary of all the controversy, accepted the winning pro-Tory ticket as valid. A budding quarrel over the returns for delegates to the state ratifying convention was also quietly resolved. An inquiry was ruled unnecessary as both factions, despite their differences, welcomed the new federal Constitution. After this, though bad feelings undoubtedly remained, election fervor cooled down. The state contests in 1788 and 1789, including the selection of Delaware's one representative to Congress, were conducted without incident.[40]

In New Jersey, from the very onset strong factional differences existed between "Cosmopolitan" West Jersey and "Localist" East Jersey. Men in the latter region firmly supported a relentless prosecution of the war, stiff measures against Loyalists, and large issues of paper money. Their West Jersey opponents tended to take a more moderate approach toward these matters. Despite the disagreements political clashes involving the two sides rarely extended beyond the legislature. Following the war, hotly-contested elections were uncommon in most counties, and campaigning was relatively limited. Where competition did take place it was often based on local questions, though in some cases it did concern statewide issues. Perhaps the hardest-fought contests occurred in Burlington and Hunterdon counties, close to the central part of the state. Conflicts between ardent Whigs and the so-called "disaffected" (Tories and their sympathizers) led to several disputed races in Burlington in the early 1780s. On one occasion there, in 1783, militia groups openly harassed voters coming to the polls. A few years later, the balloting in Hunterdon was carried on in such an irregular manner that more than two hundred petitioners demanded that the results be set aside. Such episodes were unusual, however, as most elections in the state proceeded in a calm, orderly fashion.[41]

Even the quest for seats in the state ratifying convention in the fall of 1787 was rather uneventful. Newspapers published few articles on the subject and, in general, the candidates engaged in little electioneering. Clearly, the vast majority of Jerseyites from both factions favored the new federal Constitution. While none of the returns has been preserved, it is doubtful whether there was much division in the balloting. Yet, a year later, the long-standing sectional rivalry finally went public. The election of representatives to the first Congress somehow ignited the greatest struggle the state had ever seen, and one of the bitterest anywhere in this period. The West Jersey group known as the "Junto" stopped at nothing to gain votes, and the East Jersey side acted in much the same manner. The campaign was characterized not by discussion of real issues but by attacks on personalities and "appeals to sectional jealousy." The contest was plagued by corruption at every turn, and although the easterners protested against the final verdict, the western-dominated upper house ruled the Junto ticket victorious and the judgment was allowed to stand.[42]

Statewide elections in New York were relatively dull and one-sided during the war period, when a significant amount of Whig unity prevailed. About the only major confrontation at the polls occurred in the initial gubernatorial race in 1777. George Clinton, backed chiefly by the yeoman farmer class in the Hudson Valley, triumphed over the wealthy Philip Schuyler, whose main voter support came from his own and neighboring tenants in the Albany area. Clinton solidified his position over the next few years and won reelection without opposition in 1780. Three years later, in

1783, he again won handily despite an effort by Schuyler and independent candidate Ephraim Paine to oust him.[43]

At the end of the war, economic and political differences among the Whigs slowly surfaced, and heated contests for the legislature started to take place, especially in New York City. The clash there pitted the prewar commercial and professional elite against the mechanics and self-made merchants. The latter favored strict measures toward one-time Tories; the former opposed them. Subsequently, the battle for seats in the house and senate spread upstate. By 1785, Henry Livingston would report: "This Country never had such a hard tryal since the Revolution between Demo[cracy] and Aristo[cracy], as it will have [at] this election. All parties are alive. . . . Letters and Lists Contending."[44] Collaboration among the Livingstons, Schuylers, and Rensselaers (the cosmopolitan group often referred to as the Anti-Clintonians) brought about a substantial victory over the governor's faction (the localist-minded Clintonians) in Albany and nearby areas. Within a short time the two sides were competing almost everywhere.

Easily the biggest contest of the period came in the election of members to the New York ratifying convention in the spring of 1788. Both the Anti-Clintonians, now known as Federalists, and the Clintonians, or Antifederalists, organized vigorous campaigns on a statewide basis. Included among the publications in the ensuing war of words were the Federalist Papers. The Federalists (led by Philip Schuyler and young Alexander Hamilton), having broad appeal in the mercantile community, won in New York City and in a few of the lower counties. But the Antifederalists, stressing the idea that the powers of the new government would be too great, captured a majority of seats, taking most of the upstate agrarian region. Hamilton attributed the outcome to Governor Clinton's propaganda machine. "The whole flood of official influence, accelerated by a torrent of falsehood, early gave the public opinion so violent a direction in a wrong channel that it was not possible suddenly to alter its course," he told Gouverneur Morris. Antifederal success at the polls, however, did not prevent the adoption of the Constitution, as outside circumstances influenced many delegates to accept ratification.[45]

The Antifederalists continued to control the state government for the remainder of the decade, though not without a struggle. They had to fight off many challenges to keep their hold on the legislature, and Governor Clinton himself barely won reelection in 1789 in his race with Robert Yates, a former opponent of the Constitution whom the Federalists put up against him. The Clinton forces encountered even more difficulty in the first congressional contest, ultimately having to settle for a standoff. Although the "Antis" seemed to have had a big advantage over the Federalists before the balloting, the latter won three of the six available seats.[46]

Contests in the four New England states—Massachusetts, Connecticut, New Hampshire, and Rhode Island—were somewhat less heated than those in the Middle States. The population was more homogeneous both religiously and ethnically, most inhabitants being English and, outside of Rhode Island, Congregationalist. Tories were fewer in number, which helped to hold down the amount of divisiveness. In addition, electioneering was still largely frowned upon in this region of strong traditionalism. Yet the rise of important economic issues such as the impost, high taxation, and paper money, coupled with the fact that all these states had annual popular elections of their governors and upper houses, eventually caused considerable competition in each of them.

Elections in Massachusetts did not kindle much interest until the passage of the new state constitution (1780), under which the chief executive and other high officials were to be popularly chosen. Even then, competition was limited during the next five years due to the overwhelming popularity of John Hancock, who was sent to the governor's chair each time by a wide margin. The opposing side, led by merchant James Bowdoin, continually tried to portray Hancock as incompetent and extravagant, but to little avail. Hancock remained the great, selfless patriot in the people's minds and had the capacity to dodge controversial issues which might have threatened his position. Economic questions such as the impost, heavy taxes, and the growing demand for paper money may have influenced some legislative contests, yet they did not affect the gubernatorial campaigns.[47]

In 1785, after Hancock resigned from office due to illness, the first hard-fought governor's race occurred. Bowdoin, though given strong mercantile support, managed just a small plurality in defeating former lieutenant governor Thomas Cushing and the third candidate, General Benjamin Lincoln. But the legislature gave Bowdoin the governorship. The subsequent election (1786) should have been more troublesome for Bowdoin because of the state's growing financial difficulties. Several critics, most notably Benjamin Austin (writing as "Honestus"), sharply condemned the government's hard-money policy and other alleged shortcomings. Nevertheless, the opposition remained divided, and Bowdoin was easily re-elected. The election of 1787 proved to be the biggest contest of the era in the Bay State. Angered by the worsening economic conditions which had led to Shays's Rebellion, large numbers of voters made their influence felt at the polls, rejecting the conservative policies of the incumbent administration. They not only replaced Bowdoin with Hancock, who was now well enough to resume the governorship, but also chose many new men as senators and representatives.[48]

The election of members to the state ratifying convention later that year reflected the existing political divisions. Most opponents of the Bowdoin faction and its conservative policies became Antifederalists, attacking the Constitution as aristocratic and warning against the centralization of power. The Federalists, dominated by the urban merchant class, denied that the new system would threaten individual liberties and argued that it would help bring about economic recovery. Even with their better organization and propaganda effort, it is probable that more than half of the delegates chosen, particularly those from the western counties, at first opposed ratification. Nevertheless, Federalist spokesmen at the convention succeeded in gaining John Hancock's support, and finally won enough votes to secure approval of the new document.

As the factions continued in conflict, the 1788 gubernatorial clash turned out to be another heated one. In the campaign, Hancock, moving toward a centrist position, and favored by both Federalists and moderates, triumphed over the Antifederalist candidate, Elbridge Gerry. The 1789 contest resulted in an even greater victory for Hancock. Now aligned with a new running mate, Samuel Adams, his "patriot ticket" overpowered the combination of James Bowdoin and Benjamin Lincoln, who were labelled aristocrats.[49] The first Massachusetts congressional elections in the winter of 1788–89 did not turn out as one-sided. Sharp factional rivalry, together with large districts and the need to win a full majority of the vote, caused several run-offs. The process in one area lasted three months, and in another almost five months. As the factions in some regions were not very organized, candidates of the same persuasion often ran against one another, occasionally allowing someone from the opposition to win. Despite the confusion, the Federalists, capitalizing in part on the method of districting, won six of the eight House seats allotted.[50]

Connecticut, long known as the "land of steady habits" and having experienced relative political calm for much of the provincial period, saw little competition at the ballot box at the beginning of the Revolutionary era (1776–79). This situation would continue as far as assembly elections were concerned, but those for statewide positions would frequently become contested over the next decade. The Localist bloc, though never gaining control of the government, did provide many obstacles for the dominant Cosmopolitan or nationalist leaders. If campaigning was not at as high a level as in some other states, the vote for governor and the upper house in the 1780s came out exceedingly close in a number of instances.

During the first few years of the war, longtime governor Jonathan Trumbull and his deputy governor Matthew Griswold had no formal opposition and won easily on each occasion. In fact, in 1776 and 1778, support for the two was so unanimous that the legislature did not bother to make an official count of the ballots. Virtually every member of the upper house was perennially reelected too. Starting in 1780, however, the nationalist-minded wartime leaders lost their solid backing. Trumbull, rumored to be connected with illegal trading ventures, failed to receive a clear majority of the popular vote, and retained his post only by choice of the assembly. Major issues such as the impost, high taxation, price regulation, and treatment of Tories caused increasing problems for the aging Trumbull from 1781 to 1783. Only once, in 1782, did he obtain a popular majority, and then just barely—winning by a margin of nineteen votes.[51]

The Localist opposition to the fiscally conservative administration became more powerful and open after this; a large group of dissidents held a convention in Middletown in the latter part of 1783 and organized a competing ticket. Nonetheless, at the election of 1784, many of the convention-backed candidates for the legislature were soundly defeated, though Griswold, who had replaced the retiring Trumbull, was unable to get a majority vote. As his predecessor had frequently done, he won the governorship only with the aid of the assembly. The Localist group fared somewhat better in 1785 despite Griswold's continuance in the governorship.

The appointment of several councillors to the superior court paved the way for two of their leaders, James Wadsworth and Erastus Wolcott, to enter the upper house. The next year (1786), the Anti-nationalists, as they were sometimes called, preserved their gains. Although Wadsworth was originally left out of the council, the retirement of Griswold and the accession of Samuel Huntington to the governor's chair left a spot available for him.

Connecticut's election in the spring of 1787 was perhaps its most vigorously fought one of the decade. Localist opponents of the Constitutional Convention were successful in numerous races for the upper and lower houses, and almost stopped Oliver Wolcott, a staunch nationalist, from becoming lieutenant governor. But a year later (1788), the supporters of the Constitution known as Federalists began to take over. First, through the use of "high-pressure propaganda," they captured most of the places in the constitutional ratifying convention. Then, following a similar plan in the regular statewide election, they ousted many Localists or Antifederalists, most notably James Wadsworth, from their seats in the legislature. The number of genuine contests now started to diminish as the Federalists quickly took control of all state offices, including the entire delegation to the first Congress.[52]

Little is known about New Hampshire elections during the Revolutionary war (1776–83). While some geographical division existed, no real factions developed statewide. Local competition for a place in the legislature may have occurred at times, yet the vast majority of seats was probably uncontested. By the mid-1780s, however, the new state constitution went into operation, and the popular choice of governor (at first called the president) seems to have sparked considerable personal rivalry, which soon led to vigorous clashes at the polls.[53]

Actually, the initial election for the governor's chair did not provide much of a challenge, as most state officials agreed that the aging leader Meshech Weare should have the top post the first year. But after Weare's retirement in early 1785, a wide-open battle immediately developed. Four candidates declared themselves to be in the race: John Sullivan, the conservative state attorney general; George Atkinson, former speaker of the house; and merchant politicians John and Woodbury Langdon. Although Atkinson obtained a plurality in the popular vote, he did not have the required majority, so the legislature gave the nod to John Langdon, who had been a stronger patriot.

The next three gubernatorial contests (1786–88) were principally between John Langdon, whose main support lay among the inland towns, and John Sullivan, who drew his strength from the more commercial coastal areas. In 1786, Sullivan, still remembered for his wartime service, and now cultivating his image as "a man of the people," won by a big margin. Yet, by the following year (1787), Sullivan's policies, especially his failure to solve growing economic problems, had gotten him into trouble with the electors, so that Langdon gained a higher popular vote. Nevertheless, Langdon did not receive a full majority, and since Sullivan had been successful in putting down civil disturbances, the latter was given the top office again by the house and senate. In the election of 1788, Langdon finally did acquire the needed 50 percent (though only by a single vote), thus attaining the coveted spot on his own for the first time.[54]

The choosing of delegates to the state ratifying convention that same year stimulated much less enthusiasm than had the previous gubernatorial race. Parties were not well organized and campaigning, while heavy in some areas, was light in others. The vote produced an Antifederal majority, but the body, after deliberating for a time and failing to reach any agreement, was adjourned. Later, upon being recalled, it changed its mind and supported the Constitution. Even less interest was shown in the subsequent designation of the first federal representatives, though it took three ballots before a full delegation—all Federalists—was chosen. The governor's race in 1789 also lacked excitement. The Langdon-Sullivan clashes had come to an end with Langdon's appointment as a United States Senator, and Sullivan was now able to return to the statehouse, winning by a slight plurality over lawyer John Pickering.[55]

Rhode Island, which had endured many high-charged elections in the late provincial period (during the Ward–Hopkins controversy), experienced few comparable moments over the first decade of the Revolutionary era. Despite some friction at times, no real factional conflict or harsh battles occurred at the polls between 1776 and 1785. Electioneering, compared to previous years, was slight. Only in the economically troubled late 1780s did the earlier style hard-fought contests temporarily return.

In 1776 and 1777, retired merchant Nicholas Cooke was easily elected governor, having no formal opposition to contend with. When Cooke left office in 1778, it was thought that a serious struggle might develop between merchant William Greene of Warwick and former deputy governor William Bradford, a Bristol lawyer. But the wartime situation limited interest, and the more popular Greene secured the top post without much difficulty. Greene was almost unanimously reelected in 1779, and while some personal rivalry could be found in the races for attorney-general and congressional delegates, factionalism was virtually nonexistent.[56]

The elections from 1780 to 1783 were somewhat more warmly contested, at least in part. Jabez Bowen, the deputy governor, failed to achieve reelection in 1780 even though Greene ran unopposed for the governorship. The following year (1781), when both Greene and Bowen were returned to office, several of the assistants (members of the upper house) lost their seats. Differences over the proposed national impost and other issues in 1782 stimulated greater competition at the ballot box, if a high incidence of legislative turnover is any indication. Nevertheless, the political situation calmed down between 1783 and 1785. At the top of the ticket, Greene and Bowen continued to be unopposed, and far fewer changes took place among the assistants and the assemblymen.[57]

In 1786, however, at a time of increasing economic hardship, when those in power sought to block any further issuances of paper money, partisan activity reached its highest level in two decades. A newly organized "Country party," supported primarily by small farmers and headed by John Collins of Newport and Daniel Owen of Gloucester, openly challenged the incumbent administration. Campaigning heavily on the currency issue—their slogan was "To Relieve the Distressed"—Collins and Owen scored a major triumph over Greene and Bowen, who had been backed by the hard-money, mercantile interests. Another heated contest was waged by the two sides in 1787, when the conservatives hoped to restore themselves to favor. But in the race against his new opponent, William Bradford, Collins was again chosen governor, this time by an even bigger margin. With the paper-money faction firmly in authority, the election of high officers in 1788 and 1789 involved much less antagonism. Collins and his associates all won easy victories at the polls. Rhode Island was still outside the Union at this point, having rejected the Constitution in an unprecedented statewide referendum. Yet, in 1790, after being threatened with secession by its commercial areas, including Providence and Newport, the state finally agreed to accept the new central government.[58]

From this survey it is evident that the departure of the British and the formation of a new governmental system, along with the gradual decline of deference and the rise of factional and issue-oriented politics, led to more competitive elections in the Revolutionary era. As we have seen, the degree of competitiveness differed from section to section and even within particular areas. This resulted from various factors, such as the amount of previous political development, the relative homogeneity of the white population, the presence of distinct regional concerns, and the ability of the government to deal with its pressing issues. Generally, the states with the most diverse peoples and conflicting interests, and those which also had the greatest difficulty resolving their problems, experienced the most vigorous contests during this period.

2

The
Electorate

★ ★ ★ ★ ★ ★ ★ ★ ★ ★ ★ ★ ★ ★

The American electorate, the most fundamental part of the emerging political system, was considerably expanded during the Revolutionary era. Influenced by new thinking both at home and abroad and by strong demands for change by various disenfranchised groups and individuals, leaders in a majority of states began removing many of the long-standing restrictions upon the suffrage. Although the reforms were circumscribed to some degree and did not touch everybody, persons in several categories who had formerly been excluded from the polls could now regularly cast their ballots on election day.

To be sure, the franchise was already quite extensive in the late provincial period. Not all obstacles to eligibility before 1776 were insurmountable. Despite the existence of stringent regulations regarding race, religion, residence, citizenship, and especially property holding, a major part of the adult white males—perhaps 50 to 80 percent—had acquired the suffrage. Nonetheless, a substantial number of free white men (20 to 50 percent), not to mention other segments of the population such as blacks and women, failed to meet all the requirements. Noncitizens and recent settlers in a particular colony were generally denied the vote. Members of minority religious sects found themselves barred in certain regions. Clearest in evidence among the unqualified males were those of little property—agricultural laborers and tenant farmers in the rural areas, and unskilled workers in the large coastal cities.[1]

The limitations upon entry into the electorate were not subjected to much inquiry until shortly before independence. Prior to that time most political spokesmen staunchly defended the existing suffrage qualifications and expressed no desire to change the status quo. Wishing to preserve harmony in society, they repeatedly cited the dangers of allowing a religious dissenter or a man without property to vote. Religious dissidents, they said, might be welded into a formidable opposition party, while the unpropertied could be manipulated by some artful demagogue; either group was capable of causing havoc. Women, slaves, indentured servants, noncitizens, and youths under twenty-one were rejected for similar reasons. All of them allegedly lacked the independence and moral qualities deemed essential in a voter. Yet, in spite of this widespread exclusion, those people ruled ineligible apparently acquiesced in their own disenfranchisement. Few, if any, ever protested or publicly called for an extension of the suffrage.[2]

In the 1760s and 1770s, however, the new constraints placed upon the colonists by the British stimulated rethinking about the role of the governed and the rights an individual ought to possess. England's increasing denial of fundamental liberties led some Americans to espouse the theory that mankind had certain natural and inalienable rights. Soon, a number of writers began applying this idea to conditions at home, questioning political inequity within the thirteen provinces, not just in the imperial relationship. As the historian Chilton Williamson has emphatically stated: "The period leading up to the Revolution, as well as the Revolution itself, was the turning point in the conscious democratization of ideas about the suffrage and in the actual liberalization of the colonial suffrage laws. These repercussions of the Revolutionary crisis were logical outcomes of a movement resting upon a philosophy of natural rights."[3]

In developing a new attitude toward suffrage rights Americans were influenced not only by their own situation, but by the provocative views being put forth by political reformers in Britain. Several native-born critics of England's governing system had, at this very same time, been pressing for changes in their country's voting requirements. Joseph Priestley, for example, in his *Essay on the First Principles of Government* (1768), had proposed a major broadening of the franchise, claiming that "in certain natural rights all men are equal."[4] James Burgh's lengthy tract *Political Disquisitions* (1774) also included a plea for suffrage expansion, complaining that the poor paid heavy taxes, yet had no share in determining the law givers.[5] Though the arguments of Priestley, Burgh, and others did not find acceptance in Parliament, these authors' demands for revision would have considerable impact in the New World, where their works were read with great interest.[6]

Spurred by the efforts of the English radicals and by the ideals surrounding the struggle with the mother country, several Americans began challenging some of the traditional restrictions upon the suffrage, particularly the notion of heavy property qualifications. James Otis, the well-known Massachusetts lawyer and strong defender of the colonists' position, stated that each individual by nature had "his life and liberty," and should have the right to vote regardless of whether he owned property.[7] Benjamin Franklin, while colonial agent in England in 1770, wrote that the franchise should be "the common right of [all] freemen."[8] Petitioners in Salem County, New Jersey, a few years later, ridiculed the idea that land ownership necessarily gave someone the capacity to vote. "We cannot conceive," they said, that "the wise Author of our Existence ever designed that a certain quantity of the Earth on which we tread should be annexed to Man to Compleat his dignity and fit him for society."[9] One New Jersey resident, in advocating reform, argued that if poor people continued to be excluded from choosing representatives, they ought to be exempted from paying taxes as well.[10]

The majority of men in authority, primarily from well-to-do backgrounds, did not readily embrace these views. Most Patriot leaders still thought that political participation should be reserved for those who had a "common interest with, and an attachment to the community." The right to vote, therefore, should be limited to individuals with a financial "stake in society," for they alone could make competent, reasonable judgments. They alone could be trusted in making decisions involving the use and disposal of property. As Edmund Pendleton of Virginia told Thomas Jefferson, "The right of Suffrage . . . I think . . . should be confined to those of fixed Permanent property, who cannot suddenly remove without injury to that property."[11] John Adams warned John Sullivan of New Hampshire that giving propertyless persons the vote would open the way to corruption and demagoguery. "Very few men who have no property," he exclaimed, "have any judgment of their own. They talk and vote as they are directed by some man of property who has attached their minds to his interest." The removal of property qualifications, he added, would "confound and destroy all distinctions, and prostrate all ranks to one common level."[12]

In spite of their wish to maintain existing barriers, leaders in many of the colonies saw the pressure for suffrage reform mounting rapidly. Furthermore, these officials soon realized that it was necessary to have as large a part of the population behind them as possible if they were to keep the British at arm's length. Thus, they began making concessions, allowing those males who did not meet the regular requirements to participate in the election of delegates to the various provincial congresses in late 1775 and early 1776. But such moves brought only partial satisfaction to the unenfranchised. As the moment of independence neared, quite a few of them, especially young soldiers, started demanding that the lower qualifications become permanent. Members of several militia groups insisted that if they were going to fight for the new nation they ought to be given full political equality regardless of their economic status. A petition by a number of privates in a Pennsylvania military association firmly declared: "[It] is highly reasonable that all Persons (not being Mercenaries) who expose their Lives in Defence of a Country, should be admitted to the Enjoyment of all Rights and Privileges of a Citizen of that Country which they have defended and protected."[13]

The movement for suffrage expansion was perhaps strongest in the cities of New York and Philadelphia, home of many individuals without the vote, and also major centers of political activism. The drive to extend voting rights in New York City was sponsored by the Committee of Mechanics, successor to the Sons of Liberty, which made frequent appeals for a broader franchise. In Philadelphia, a similar group, the Mechanic Association, pushed hard for modifications, as did key figures in the "radical" party: James Cannon, Timothy Matlack, and Dr. Thomas Young. These men argued that if all taxpayers in English towns and boroughs were enfranchised, that is, each inhabitant who "paid his scot and bore his lot," why not Americans of the same rank and condition? They also reiterated the views of the military volunteers; an essay by one of them in the *Pennsylvania Packet* asserted that "every man in the country who manifests a disposition to venture his all for the defence of its Liberty should have a voice in its Councils."[14]

Although most advocates of suffrage reform operated in a peaceful manner, some went beyond mere words to demonstrate their desire for change. The greatest outbreak of militant activity occurred in eastern Maryland, where disenfranchisement was particularly widespread. At the polling places in several counties in the summer of 1776, numerous unqualified males, many of them soldiers, defied the authorities and sought to vote, saying they would no longer bear arms if denied. In a few cases the regular election judges were forcibly removed and their replacements permitted all taxpayers to participate. When the judge's assistant in Anne Arundel County attempted to uphold the normal property standards and started reading the rules out loud, a crowd began shouting, "Pull him down, he shall not read, we will not hear it, and if you do not stop and let every free man vote that carries arms we will pull the house down from under the judges."[15]

Not all states were affected by these rumblings. Some, which already had relatively low voting requirements, did not experience any protest and showed no interest in making alterations. Here, if new laws or constitutional voting clauses were enacted, they contained basically the same qualifications as the old. Yet elsewhere vigorous appeals continued to be heard, causing a majority of the former colonies to seriously contemplate reform at their conventions. Eventually seven of the original thirteen states—Pennsylvania, North Carolina, Georgia, New Hampshire, New Jersey, Maryland, and New York—though not before engaging in considerable debate on the subject, agreed to include more liberal voting provisions in their constitutions.

The ideas behind the proposed revisions, however, did not represent a total shift in thinking on the part of the framers. While consenting to lower the barriers of eligibility, they did not really abandon the concept of "a stake in society" and adopt the democratic notion of universal manhood suffrage. These men simply broadened their view of what constituted communal interest, no longer limiting it to the ownership of substantial amounts of property. The absence of any complete break can be seen in the fact that each of the states retained some type of taxpaying or minimal property standard, implicitly denying the vote to the idle and profligate. There was little desire to give voting privileges to the poor who, it was felt, would pay scant regard to the rights of property "because they have nothing to lose." The belief that an elector should be independent and possess certain moral qualities was clearly reaffirmed. The new enactments, therefore, did not enfranchise everyone. Nevertheless, many males did gain their fundamental political rights for the first time as a result of all the modifications made.[16]

In Pennsylvania, where the greatest movement to extend the franchise had developed, a provincial conference in June, 1776, resolved that the existing fifty acre/fifty pound requirement be disregarded in the election of members to the state's constitutional convention. Then, at the convention itself in September, 1776, advocates of a broader suffrage, led by James Cannon and Timothy Matlack, easily overcame the opponents of change. They soon made Pennsylvania the first state to remove property ownership as a qualification, granting the vote to all adult white male taxpayers. One slight concession was given to landowners, for it was decided that sons of freeholders who were over twenty-one "shall be entitled to vote although they have not payed taxes."[17] This last measure can also be interpreted as a step toward full democracy, since certain individuals could now vote without themselves having a direct financial stake in the community.

North Carolina went almost as far in reducing property qualifications, though it encountered much more resistance. Instructions to several representatives to the provincial congress at Hillsborough (August 1775), calling for lower suffrage levels, were not favorably acted upon. Proposals to abolish the freehold requirement at the congress in Halifax (April 1776) also met with rejection. In each case, conservatives succeeded in holding back attempts at reform, but then their support began to weaken. Finally, some months later, state leaders worked out a compromise for the new constitution by creating two levels of eligibility, a concept later admired by James Madison. While only fifty-acre freeholders could elect persons to the senate, taxpaying freemen could vote for members of the assembly. Since taxation was by poll, all adult males except "sons living under their paternal roof, apprentices, slaves, and indentured servants" were enfranchised for house elections.[18]

In Georgia, where a fifty-acre landholding requirement had been the rule in the colonial period, the push for reform began early. Many delegates to the provincial congress in July, 1775, were elected at local meetings whose participants included non-landowners. This congress gave all taxpayers the vote for future gatherings of this type, and in the following year permitted them to choose representatives to the state's constitutional convention. However, the convention officials themselves retreated a bit in drawing up the suffrage provision for the constitution. The completed document set up a ten-pound property qualification, yet it allowed men in any "mechanic trade" to vote without their necessarily being property owners, thus enabling most adult white males to qualify.[19]

New Hampshire, which had a fifty-pound property requirement in the provincial era, also witnessed much clamor for change. As a result, the voting qualification was reduced to twenty pounds for the election of the provincial congress in December, 1775. During the next several months many criticized this move as not having gone far enough and, in the first draft of the state constitution in late 1776, a taxpaying standard was established. Conservatives then rallied to strike down this provision, claiming that it gave the propertyless the potential to overthrow the propertied class. A revised version, appearing some time afterward, permitted taxpayers to choose the lower house but confined the designation of the upper house to freeholders or men with property worth one hundred pounds. Yet this statement was eliminated, too—through the efforts of the opposing liberal side. Eventually, the conservatives relented; in the final document, framed in 1782, those paying just a poll tax were made eligible for all elections, leaving very few males outside the fold.[20]

New Jersey, having required a substantial freehold suffrage in earlier years, faced even greater demands for change, though the results were not as far-reaching as some people desired. In fact, at the outset, almost no progress occurred at all. Numerous petitions for a taxpayer qualification were set aside by the provincial congress in late 1775 and even more limited revisions kept being postponed. Nevertheless, reform here was inevitable. In early 1776, the congress, by a margin of nine counties to four, moved to end the landholding requirement and to extend the franchise to those individuals possessing the equivalent of fifty pounds, currency or proclamation money. Subsequently, the state constitution drawn up in the summer of 1776 contained this same provision, giving the vote to "all the inhabitants . . . of full age . . . worth fifty Pounds, Proclamation money, clear estate."[21]

Property qualifications in Maryland came under very sharp attack at the time of independence. Advocates of suffrage reform, often ignoring traditional regulations, achieved considerable success in getting their candidates elected to the state constitutional convention. In consequence, many of the convention delegates were committed to a much broader franchise than the existing one (fifty acres/forty pounds personal estate). During the debates they proposed reducing the property level to just five pounds, but the plan was defeated by three votes. They then introduced a resolution calling for the elimination of all property requirements, though this too was blocked by a small margin. Ultimately, the conservatives managed to keep the long-standing fifty-acre freehold; yet they agreed to lessen the forty-pound-sterling property alternative to thirty pounds current money, which actually cut the amount needed for eligibility in half.[22]

People in New York expressed much less sentiment for suffrage reform than those in Maryland. Yet, for a time, it appeared that modifications might be greater there. At the state constitutional convention in 1777, the original draft of the franchise provision gave the right to vote for the lower house to all freeholderes and taxpayers resident in the counties. The convention delegates, influenced by the conservative arguments put forth by Robert R. Livingston and Gouverneur Morris, eventually drew back from such a sweeping change. Still, the property qualifications established for assembly elections were now reduced in comparison to the levels of the provincial period—from a fifty-pound to a twenty-pound freehold. In addition, tenants paying an annual rent of forty shillings were able to vote for house members. But a dual system was introduced here, and the election of senators was placed beyond the reach of the average person, being confined to one hundred-pound freeholders.[23]

In Massachusetts, it seemed as though suffrage expansion would take place at this juncture too, but in the end the minimum standard was raised rather than lowered. All adult males in the summer of 1776 were permitted to vote on whether the legislature should prepare a new constitution. Then, the first draft of the constitution, submitted in 1778, allowed all taxpayers to elect the house of representatives and the governor, restricting only the selection of the senate to men worth sixty pounds. This document was subsequently rejected by the towns for several reasons, none of them related to the voting provisions. The final version, approved in 1780, somehow contained a higher qualification, as sixty pounds personal property was now necessary for designating all state officials. The new regulation was defended on the grounds that the only ones disenfranchised would be young men living on their parents' estate just entering into business, or those "whose Idleness of Life and profligacy of manners will forever bar them from acquiring and possessing Property."

Over forty Bay State communities sharply criticized the enactment, seeing it either as an infringement of natural rights or against the principles of no taxation without representation. Some directly questioned the validity of the above-stated rationale. The town of Mansfield, for example, asked: "How many young men neither profligate nor idle persons, for some years must be debarred from that privilege [of voting]? How many sensible, honest and naturally industrious men, by numberless misfortunes, never acquire and possess property to the value of 60 pounds?" Despite the protest, the higher standard remained in force. Actually, it is doubtful whether the small increase (17 percent) represented much of an upward shift at all, since the old fifty-pound requirement was in sterling, the new one in less valuable paper currency.[24]

South Carolina and Virginia experienced only minor changes in the franchise during the Revolutionary era. The liberal suffrage provisions in the South Carolina constitution (1778) were practically the same as those in the provincial period. Voters had to possess a fifty-acre freehold or pay a tax equivalent to that on fifty acres of land, the latter clause modifying to a small degree the previous twenty-shilling tax level.[25] Virginia, at its constitutional convention in 1776, resolved that the old freehold qualification be kept in its present form. Edmund Randolph later noted that limiting political participation to substantial freeholders was understandable after more than one hundred years of the practice. "It was not recollected," he added, "that a hint was uttered in contravention of this principle. There can be no doubt that if it had been it would have perished under discussion."[26] Nine years afterward, in 1785, Virginia did reduce its requirements slightly. While retaining the freehold standard of twenty-five acres of improved land, it lowered the amount of unimproved land needed from one hundred acres to fifty acres.[27]

The three other states, Delaware, Rhode Island, and Connecticut, made no change in their suffrage laws whatsoever. Delaware, when enacting its new constitution in 1776, evidently believed there was no need to alter the fifty-acre freehold or the forty-pound personal property limit. The document simply stated that the rules of eligibility should "remain as at present."[28] In Rhode Island, which did not adopt a new constitution, voting qualifications never became an issue at this time. The former requirement—that free men possess real estate valued at forty pounds or which rented for forty shillings per annum—was deemed satisfactory.[29] Connecticut, working under the same standards, did make one small attempt at reform. In 1779, a bill was introduced into the assembly requesting that all taxpayers be enfranchised. Although the measure was debated briefly, it did not achieve passage, and the old law continued in operation as before.[30]

The impact of the new constitutions and other legislation upon the size of the electorate is difficult to ascertain. Before 1790, no exact figures regarding qualified voters were ever made public. In fact, most states never bothered with an official count. However, a rough survey seems to indicate that where requirements were altered very little, the proportion of eligibles remained about the same. On the other hand, those states initiating major revisions saw their numbers expand, sometimes by more than just a few percentage points.[31]

Pennsylvania, which made the greatest innovation, saw the widest extension of any voting class in this period. The new taxpaying qualification enlarged the body of electors anywhere from 10 to 40 percent, depending upon the locale. The biggest increases occurred in the older, established areas such as Bucks, Chester, and Philadelphia counties where no more than 50 to 60 percent qualified previously; the more recently settled frontier regions, already having considerable enfranchisement, experienced a smaller climb. Overall, about 90 percent of the adult white males were now taxpaying freemen. This is corroborated by a contemporary estimate in 1787 claiming upwards of 70,000 eligible voters, when the census showed the state had approximately 80,000 adult white men.[32]

North Carolina and Georgia, having introduced requirements that were easily met, also witnessed a substantial rise in the number of eligible voters. A sizable majority of the white males (perhaps 70 percent) may have been freeholders in each of the two erstwhile colonies prior to 1776, but the addition of the newly enfranchised elements (taxpayers in the former, mechanics and ten-pound property holders in the latter) meant that very few white men were still excluded. The same situation characterized postwar New Hampshire. Under the new taxpaying qualification practically every adult male possessed the right of suffrage. As evidence of this, a writer in the *New Hampshire Mercury* in 1785 noted that the "worthy lowerclass of people" was now participating in town election meetings. In all three states around 90 percent could go to the polls during the Confederation era.[33]

New Jersey also recorded significant gains. A recent sampling of tax lists from the mid-1770s discloses that roughly 50 to 75 percent of the adult white male inhabitants were freeholders. But the removal of the landholding criterion and the establishment of fifty pounds proclamation money as the minimum requirement expanded the suffrage much further—probably close to 90 percent. Richard McCormick, in his illuminating study of New Jersey voting, points out that in the post-Revolutionary period the legislature did not receive a single petition for any additional extension of the franchise. Moreover, in only one of the many disputed elections in these years was the property qualification a major issue. After assessing the data, McCormick concludes that "the percentage of men who could not swear to being worth fifty pounds, lawful money, must have been extremely small, especially when the currency depreciation of the times is taken into consideration."[34]

South Carolina, Delaware, and Massachusetts, which did not alter their requirements much, already had fairly sizable electorates. Tax lists from several South Carolina parishes in the 1780s show that more than 80 percent of the adult white males could vote.[35] Election returns and other data from Delaware indicate that an equivalent number had the requisite property to participate in that state.[36] In Massachusetts, although only about 60 to 70 percent of the adult men could qualify in many seaboard towns, 80 to 90 percent were eligible in most rural sections, as figures gathered separately by Robert E. Brown and Robert J. Taylor amply demonstrate. Indeed, the contemporary chronicler of political activities in the Bay State, George Minot, declared in 1788, "So small are the qualifications of voters that scarce a single man is excluded."[37]

The situation for prospective electors in Maryland was not quite the same but there was a growing resemblance. While no more than half of the adult white males were landholders in the early 1780s, the reduction of the visible property alternative from forty pounds sterling to thirty pounds in current money had opened the franchise to most freemen. The currency had depreciated to such a low level by the end of the decade that not too many men could have been barred on the grounds of insufficient wealth. Though figures compiled by Thornton Anderson from existing assessors' lists imply that only 64 percent could qualify in 1783, the proportion eligible must have grown larger (to over 70 percent) in the next half dozen years. The high turnouts at the polls by the year 1790—over 50 percent in some counties—attest to the rapid expansion of the vote in Maryland.[38]

The electorate in Virginia was not any bigger, as no general alternative to the freehold requirement existed. One sampling of land-ownership in seven counties by Charles Sydnor finds that only about 50 to 60 percent possessed enough acreage to qualify. A later and more extensive study by Jackson T. Main claims still lower percentages. Main asserts that not above half of those in the Piedmont and Southside were freeholders, and just 30 percent held land in the Northern Neck. Even if the number of voters was enhanced to some extent by the eligibility of long-term leaseholders and residents of a few towns, the evidence suggests that no more than 70 to 75 percent of the adult white males were able to meet the minimum standards, rather than the 85 to 90 percent estimated by Robert E. and B. Katherine Brown in their work on the Old Dominion.[39]

New York's electorate was probably even smaller than Virginia's. Despite the addition of twenty-pound freeholders and forty-shilling renters, those eligible to vote for the lower house comprised just 58 percent of the adult white males and 70.7 percent of the heads of families in 1790, according to the thorough analysis by Alfred Young. Furthermore, just 28.9 percent of the men could select members of the upper house. While all yeoman farmers, merchants and professionals were eligible, many laborers, tenant farmers, and sons of yeomen and tenant farmers remained excluded. In New York City, where the freemanship had once been easily obtainable, it seems that only about 60 percent of the adult men could now legally qualify.[40]

In Rhode Island, a state that retained its old suffrage laws, statistics compiled by Joel Cohen from a number of country towns reveal almost three-fourths of the adult males could meet the minimum property requirements. His study of extant valuations of estates and rateable polls in 1778 shows 76 percent could qualify in Coventry, 65 percent in Exeter, and 71 percent in Gloucester. After

adding valuation lists for Richmond (79 percent) and South Kingstown (77 percent), which are somewhat less precise about the types
of property owned, he concludes that eligibility for the freemanship
approximated 74 percent. The proportion of the total who actually
became freemen, however, was much smaller. As in the provincial
period, an oath was necessary for qualification, and it would appear
that only four-fifths of the men able to ever bothered to take the
oath. A legislative report issued in 1788 mentions the existence of
roughly 7,000 bona fide freemen, the equivalent of 60 to 70 percent
of the adult males.[41]

An even lower percentage of adult males became freemen in
Connecticut, where oath taking was also required for eligibility. A
survey made by Philip H. Jordan of the number of freemen sworn
in twenty-eight towns indicates that an average of only 42 percent
subscribed to the oath, whereas perhaps as many as 75 percent
could have qualified. The data provide an interesting sectional
variation as well. About 44.5 percent of the men in eighteen western communities sought freeman status, while just 37.5 percent of
those in ten eastern locales followed that course. It is possible that
these figures, often based on calculations from the war years,
underestimate the proportion of voters. Yet it is doubtful that,
overall, more than 60 percent of the adult males could cast ballots
in Connecticut.[42]

Therefore, in the thirteen states as a whole, the electorate, as a
result of the changes in property qualifications, probably expanded
from a range of 50 to 80 percent in the late provincial period to
about 60 to 90 percent by the close of the Revolutionary era. (This
actually represents more than a 10 percent rise, as many states were
now near the upper rather than the lower end of the span.) Pennsylvania, North Carolina, Georgia, New Hampshire, and New Jersey
had the highest degrees of eligibility, around the 90 percent mark;
South Carolina, Delaware, and Massachusetts were not far behind,
with upwards of 80 percent; Maryland and Virginia at 70 to 75 percent came next, followed by New York and Rhode Island, somewhere between 60 and 70 percent; Connecticut found itself lodged
at the bottom, in the vicinity of 60 percent.

Of course, major variations often existed within each state,
including some areas where the size of the electorate was clearly
declining. As land in parts of New England was being subdivided
into smaller tracts, proportionately fewer men achieved eligibility

with each ensuing generation. Charles Grant's study of the town of Kent, Connecticut, shows that whereas 79 percent of the resident adult males could qualify for the freemanship in 1777, only 63 percent could do so in 1796.[43] Kenneth Lockridge in his work on land-holding patterns in eastern Massachusetts estimates that in certain older settlements the group of men satisfying the minimum suffrage standard in 1790 may have diminished by as much as 30 percent compared to the pre-Revolutionary era.[44] Nevertheless, due to the reduced requirements and to the opening up of new lands, the voting class throughout most of the nation was becoming larger.

The enactment of relatively low property qualifications on the state level made it certain that, when the federal Constitution was being drawn up in 1787, no higher standard would be established for electing members to the United States House of Representatives. As James Wilson of the convention's Committee of Detail put it, "It would be very hard and disagreeable for the same persons, at the same time, to vote for representatives in the state legislature and to be excluded from a vote for those in the national legislature."[45] To be sure, some conservatives such as Gouverneur Morris and John Dickinson wished to introduce a freehold qualification, fearing the growth of a propertyless and untrustworthy industrial working class. But Oliver Ellsworth of Connecticut correctly surmised that the people would "not readily subscribe to the national constitution if it should subject them to be disfranchised."[46] Perhaps Benjamin Franklin summed up the situation best when he declared that virtue and public spirit had flourished in America, where most men had the vote, and had declined in England, where most men did not.[47]

Property qualifications were not the only ones to undergo change. While property standards were being lowered, religious requirements were reduced even further, to a point where almost all Christians could vote. Only the Jews in certain states remained legally outside the fold. Prior to the Revolution, at least five provinces—Virginia, New York, Maryland, Rhode Island, and South Carolina—had officially barred Roman Catholics or popish recusants from the polls. Influenced by the growth of religious tolerance, the framers of the new state constitutions and other legislation brought an end to most Catholic exclusion. New York's constitution, though calling for immigrants to take an oath renouncing all foreign allegiances in matters ecclesiastical as well as civil, contained no religious tests for persons already citizens. The Maryland Bill of Rights stated that all men "professing the Christian religion" were "equally entitled to protection in their religious liberty," implying full suffrage for Catholics. South Carolina's constitution of 1778 allowed the vote to all those who acknowledged "the being of a God," and believed in a "future state of rewards." The Rhode Island legislature in 1783 decreed that "all the Rights and Privileges of the Protestant citizens . . . be fully extended to Roman Catholics." Virginia's constitution of 1776 had retained the earlier restrictions, but they were repealed by implication in 1785 in section three of Jefferson's statute for religious freedom. Although the number of voters added by the new religious clauses was not very extensive, the men of the Revolutionary generation established a principle which would have profound meaning in the future, when many non-Protestant immigrants started arriving in America.[48]

Racial requirements for voting were also being altered at this point. Several states allowed free Negroes to possess the franchise for the first time, though often due to inadvertence, confusion, and haste in constitution-making, rather than to conscious design. In Pennsylvania, North Carolina, and New York, free blacks became members of the electorate on the same terms as whites. (Of course, the latter state's property qualification continued to serve as a barrier to many.) Maryland's constitution (1776) permitted voting for the lower house without color discrimination, but a statute in 1783 denied the ballot to anyone manumitted after that date.[49] Massachusetts experienced considerable debate over the political status of non-whites when its state constitution was being formulated in the late 1770s. After the first draft, which excluded blacks, Indians, and mulattoes, was made public, Reverend William Gordon, a proponent of suffrage for all colored peoples, wrote in the *Independent Chronicle:* "Would it not be ridiculous, inconsistent and unjust to exclude freemen from voting . . . though otherwise qualified, because their skins are black, tawny or reddish? Why not disqualified for being long-nosed, short-faced, or higher or lower than five feet nine? A black, tawny or reddish skin is not so unfavorable a hue to the genuine son of liberty as a tory complection."[50] Blacks themselves pointed out that their exclusion was no different than the British refusal of American rights. If the Massachusetts Constitution approved in 1780 did not specifically give the franchise to persons of color, the lack of any distinction among males in the voting provision was interpreted to mean that such individuals could take part. That blacks actually did go to the polls is confirmed in a letter from Jeremy Belknap of Boston in 1788. "The negroes of sufficient property vote in town-meetings," he said. "Prince Hall, Grand Master of the Black Lodge, constantly votes for Governour and Representatives; so do some others."[51]

While voting restrictions were being lifted for certain groups, women continued to be barred from the suffrage, and in a more decisive manner than earlier. There was but one exception: the state of New Jersey. The provision in its constitution that "all the inhabitants . . . of full age . . . worth fifty Pounds" could vote was interpreted to include unmarried women otherwise qualified.[52] Although not too many took advantage of this opportunity, some New Jersey women did exercise their franchise rights until the year 1807 when, after several allegations of fraud, an amendment was passed which took away the privilege. Certain other states, beginning with New York in 1777, had made sure that women would not be permitted to vote by placing the word *male* in their constitution's voting statement. The reasons for excluding women from the polls were not usually spelled out in print. But the statement of Theophilus Parsons of Massachusetts in the *Essex Result* (1778) probably well expressed the prevailing view. "Women what age soever they are of, are . . . considered as not having a sufficient acquired discretion; not from a deficiency in their mental powers, but from a natural tendency and delicacy of their minds, their retired mode of life, and various domestic duties. These concurring, prevent that promiscuous intercourse with the world, which is necessary to qualify them for electors."[53] Not until the middle decades of the nineteenth century would such opinions be publicly challenged.

Besides the more clear-cut restrictions placed upon women, youths and recent immigrants faced greater legal barriers than before. Age and citizenship requirements, often customary in the provincial period, were generally included in the new state constitutions. All the states demanded that a voter be a citizen and that he be twenty-one years old, or of "full age," as in the constitutions of New York and New Jersey. In addition, residency was now formally required in several states. Pennsylvania and Delaware stipulated that electors be a resident for one year, though the minimum in

Georgia and New York was just six months. New York was the only state which specifically called for residence within the same county, and Massachusetts the only one which requested habitation within the same town. These regulations must have been generally acceptable, for neither the age nor the residence provisions was accompanied by any significant debate when put into law.[54]

Perhaps the most controversial voting restrictions to be enacted during this period, though temporary in nature, were the so-called test laws. At the beginning of the war, most of the states adopted statutes requiring individuals to sever all connections with England and declare their loyalty to the American cause. Those who refused to take this oath of allegiance were often denied the vote; five states—New York, Rhode Island, Maryland, North Carolina, and South Carolina—directly disfranchised Loyalists. Some states even kept these laws in force long after the war's conclusion. In Pennsylvania, where Quakers and other neutrals had been deprived of the franchise beginning in 1777, the Constitutionalist party continued to support the Test Act until 1786, when its Republican opponents finally succeeded in removing it. New York retained its ban on former Tories until 1788. But with its elimination test laws finally came to an end.[55]

Thus, by the close of the Revolutionary era, most adult white males and even a few others had obtained the elective franchise. Property qualifications had been reduced, religious requirements practically abandoned, and racial restrictions removed in some cases. While there was still much room for additional reform, especially for women and blacks, significant steps had already been taken to permit greater participation in America's political life. The new nation, though not yet in adherence with a concept of every citizen having the vote, had inaugurated a trend toward universal white manhood suffrage and had opened the possibility of further broadening of the eligibility limits.

3

The Candidates

The candidates in the Revolutionary period continued to be a major element in an election. Although factional and issue-based politics was increasing, the candidates in many cases still occupied the center stage. But the type of individual becoming a candidate and the rules governing this no longer remained the same. During the provincial era, the persons who stood for public posts were primarily the rich and well-born, who had to satisfy strict requirements in regard to property holding, religion, and several other matters.[1] However, the rise of democratic ideas on the eve of independence led to a reduction in numerous qualifications, which, together with changing attitudes, often inspired different kinds of men—those of less affluent backgrounds—to seek election. Even though a good many members of the gentleman class kept on running for office, more and more places were eventually filled by these "new men."

The striking departures made in the realm of officeholding were closely connected to other political changes occurring at the time. Just as a number of Americans had begun questioning the restrictions upon who could vote, some started questioning the restrictions upon who could hold office. They directed their main assault at the existence of high property qualifications, which in certain colonies stood at five hundred to one thousand pounds and excluded a large segment of the population. As early as the summer of 1775, the people of Mechlenburg County, North Carolina, instructed their representatives to the provincial congress to call for the removal of property qualifications for members of the assembly. The following year, petitioners from a group of sixteen New Hampshire towns requested the elimination of property requirements for all offices.[2]

Several writers reinforced this demand, strongly rejecting the view that property ownership should be the chief prerequisite for officeholding. Property qualifications, they said, would inevitably bring forward the type of candidate whose main goal was to further his own private interest. The author of the pamphlet *The People the Best Governors* (1776), in fact, saw property standards as a definite source of corruption. Such distinctions, he declared, had the tendency to "root out virtue" and "set up the avaricious over the heads of the poor. . . . Let it not be said in future generations that money was made by the founders of the American states an essential qualification in the rulers of a free people." He and other spokesmen challenged the assumption that none but the most affluent were qualified to serve, stating that persons in humbler stations might be just as well suited. "Social virtue and knowledge," it was claimed, "provided the best and only necessary qualification" for a government position.[3]

Many among the "better sort" sharply disagreed, and immediately sought to refute these ideas. A Massachusetts gentleman argued that if the voters chose members of the yeomanry to important posts, the country would be at a disadvantage in the struggle against Great Britain, as such men were not at all acquainted with statecraft. He also pointed out that a representative from the lower classes would be susceptible to intense political pressure, especially in the form of executive influence. A New Yorker, labeling himself "the Watchman," added that in public life only "great abilities, or considerable property" could produce respect among the people. Anyone elected to office without these attributes, he insisted, would soon be rendered "contemptible and ridiculous." Since ability was hard to judge accurately, it was necessary that property be taken into account in determining which individuals would best serve the public. Finally, defenders of the status quo reasoned that someone who levies taxes should also be subject to them. They thought it was unfair for a poor man, without any financial stake in society, to tax a rich one.[4]

While the majority of American leaders essentially agreed with these latter statements, many of them had come to see that the earlier regulations were sometimes inequitable. Therefore, when drawing up provisions for officeholding in the new state constitutions, they made an attempt to modify the existing property qualifications to allow men who lacked extensive wealth the privilege of seeking office. As Samuel Adams later explained to the visiting

French nobleman, the Marquis de Chastellux: "It would be in vain for the people to possess the right of electing representatives, were they restrained in the choice of them to a particular class; it is necessary therefore not to require too much property as a qualification for the *representative of the people.* "[5]

The most notable reform was the easing of admission to the lower houses of the legislatures. The longtime three hundred-pound requirement in New Hampshire now dropped to one hundred pounds. The five hundred-pound sterling standard in New Jersey was changed to five hundred pounds proclamation money, half the former value. Georgia cut its five hundred-acre landowning minimum to two hundred fifty acres. Delaware introduced a simple freehold qualification with no specific amount mentioned, while Pennsylvania accepted all taxpayers, having no real property requirement whatsoever. Some states which already possessed low levels, such as Virginia and North Carolina, saw no need to make any alterations. A few did raise their requirements; Massachusetts, for example, set up a one hundred-pound freehold or two hundred-pound estate as the basic limit, more than twice the previous one. But only one state, Maryland, erected a fairly substantial barrier to assembly service—five hundred pounds real or personal property.

Since membership in the upper house was seen as involving a greater trust, property requirements for that office were generally fixed somewhat higher. Although Virginia and Delaware continued to maintain the same minimum freehold qualification in the upper as in the lower house, several states demanded that the candidate possess twice as much for a seat in the senate. New Hampshire initiated a two hundred-pound freehold, Maryland a one thousand-pound property standard, and South Carolina a two thousand-pound level. North Carolina tripled the house figure (to three hundred acres) as did Massachusetts, which established a three hundred-pound freehold or six hundred-pound personal estate. The office of governor sometimes required even more wealth: in New Hampshire five hundred pounds, in Massachusetts one thousand pounds, and in South Carolina ten thousand pounds.

Some of these amounts were certainly prohibitive as far as the average person was concerned. Less than ten percent of the male citizens in Maryland, for example, could legally qualify for the upper house. Indeed, in Maryland at its convention in 1776 and in Massachusetts a few years later, considerable opposition developed to the whole idea of property qualifications. Seventeen towns in the Bay State registered some form of protest against it. But the outcry was relatively short lived. Most people still believed that an office-holder should be independent and have a financial stake in society. Moreover, it was clear that the vast majority of public posts in America were not beyond the reach of most inhabitants who had accumulated a modest estate. Only a handful of places required ownership of property worth five hundred pounds or more; for a great many offices just a small freehold was needed.[6]

Of course, it can be argued that the new property standards for officeholding did not produce any fundamental change, as most men who wished to qualify could already do so before this time. Nevertheless, the reforms did create an atmosphere of greater equality, for they stimulated the belief that any person, even one of limited means, could rise up and ultimately get elected to a high position. This point was underscored in an address by Doctor David Ramsay of South Carolina during an Independence Day celebration in 1778. "It is the happiness of our present constitution," he said, "that all offices lie open to men of merit, of whatever rank or condition; and that even the reins of state may be held by the son of the poorest man, if possessed of abilities equal to the important station. We are no more to look up for the blessings of government to hungry courtiers or the needy dependents of British nobility."[7]

In addition to bringing down property barriers, leaders in numerous states began to eliminate religious requirements. As long as a candidate accepted Christianity, it was not as important now which particular faith he embraced. Thus, Protestant dissenters (Quakers, Baptists, etc.), formerly unable to obtain office in several colonies, no longer faced such discrimination. Roman Catholics, much more widely excluded before 1776, began to be admitted to public posts as well. The state of Maryland, which had the largest number of that faith, provided in its constitution that all persons "professing the Christian religion" were equally entitled to protection of their religious liberty. Even in places where Catholics found themselves legally disqualified the laws were often ignored. In North Carolina, Thomas Burke, an Irish Catholic, represented the state in Congress and then served as governor. Religious qualifications in Virginia and New Hampshire gradually fell into disuse by the 1780s. Curiously, the demand for religious toleration at this time did not stem from extreme democrats but rather from liberal Whigs. Some of those pressing for the most far-reaching political reforms strongly defended religious tests for officeholding, whereas more moderate spokesmen advocated their abandonment.[8]

The overall decline in religious restrictions, however, had little effect upon Jews. Most of the state constitutions continued to require that officeholders be Christian or accept the Trinity and New Testament. Few Jews complained about this, as members of the small group had no desire to hold office. Yet a petition by Rabbi Gershom Seixas to the Pennsylvania legislature in 1783 shows there was some dissatisfaction with the exclusion. "Your memorialists cannot say that the Jews are particularly fond of being representatives of the people in assembly or civil officers and magistrates in the state; but with great submission they apprehend that a clause in the constitution, which disables them to be elected by their fellow citizens to represent them in assembly is a stigma upon their nation and their religion, and it is inconsonant with the second paragraph of the said bill of rights."[9]

While property and religious tests were generally reduced, many other qualifications remained the same, and some became even more restrictive in order to protect against arbitrary or irresponsible government. Minimum age requirements for officeholders, for example, stayed at twenty-one years in the majority of cases. But a few states set up higher levels for the most important positions, evidently equating advanced age with greater trust and capability. Members of the upper house in Maryland, Delaware, and Virginia had to be "upwards of twenty-five," and the senators and governor in New Hampshire needed to be at least thirty. No other age barriers were established until a decade later, when the federal Constitution decreed that congressmen must be twenty-five, senators thirty, and the president thirty-five.[10]

Moral qualifications were retained in a number of states, often in forms basically similar to previous ones. The Pennsylvania Constitution of 1776 proclaimed that its house of representatives "shall consist of persons most noted for wisdom and virtue." Maryland's constitution called for the election of the "most wise, sensible, and discreet of the people" to the house, and "men of the most wisdom, experience, and virtue" to the senate. New York's constitution decreed that only a "wise and discreet freeholder" should be chosen governor. Massachusetts solicited public officials who would personify the principles of "piety, justice, moderation, temperance, industry, and frugality." In addition, many states during the war compelled officeholders to be loyal Americans, that is, to take an oath of allegiance to the Patriot cause.[11]

Residence requirements for officeholders were now more common than before. Just as people in America had supported actual over virtual representation during the imperial struggle, so they increasingly sought to apply this concept at home. They felt that a bona fide resident, a man who had dwelled in the community for a considerable time, would probably be more responsible and committed to its public welfare than an outsider. The terms settled upon for members of the lower house ranged from one year in Georgia, New Jersey, and North Carolina, to two years in New Hampshire and Pennsylvania, to three years in South Carolina. Higher offices sometimes required longer periods. Senators in New Hampshire and the governor of Massachusetts were supposed to have been living in their respective states for seven years. Some regulations called upon representatives to have homes in their specific district; others merely stipulated residence within the state. South Carolina was unique in enacting a much higher property qualification for non-residents (£3,500) than for residents (£2,000) seeking election to the senate.[12]

A new impediment placed in the path of elected officeholders was a limit to the number of terms they could serve. Many leaders of the time thought some form of periodic exclusion would provide "the best guard against the encroachment of power." As Richard Henry Lee told Edmund Pendleton in 1776, "abridged duration" offered a "potent means of preserving integrity in public men and for securing the Community from the dangerous ambition . . . that too often governs the human mind."[13] Influenced by the idea of rotation in office, South Carolina made sheriffs who had served two years ineligible during the next four. Pennsylvania went almost as far, confining not only sheriffs but representatives to holding office only four years in seven. Furthermore, seven of the new state constitutions restricted the number of terms a governor was allowed to serve. In Maryland and Virginia, governors elected for three terms could not serve in any of the next four. The Maryland Constitution claimed that "a long continuance in the first executive departments of power or trust is dangerous to liberty."[14]

Another stricture aimed at curtailing excess power was the widespread ban on plural officeholding. In the provincial period, the legislatures in some colonies had ejected certain placemen, but now the movement went much further. To prevent too much executive influence, almost every state constitution excluded from the lower house all persons "possessed of any post of profit under the Government." Besides those holding regular offices, such as sheriffs and tax collectors, the constitutions in Maryland and Delaware also excluded contractors for the army and navy. Some states refused to allow their military and judicial officers to be assemblymen. In Pennsylvania, no member of the legislature could hold any other position except in the militia. Even justices of the peace were barred from sitting in the house there. Among the thirteen states only South Carolina seems to have permitted placeholders to retain their seats in certain circumstances.[15]

On the whole, the enactments noted above seem to have been effective. Moreover, the higher age and residence requirements, plus the new measures limiting multiple officeholding and the number of terms one could serve, did not really hinder the rise of new men. In fact, the advent of rotation in office and the greater elimination of placemen made it easier for someone of less wealth and background to get elected, as these innovations opened up several additional positions. Actually, many more public posts had already been opened up through other means, most notably by the new state constitutions making previously appointive offices elective and by the legislature granting representation to formerly unrepresented frontier regions.

The emergence of new types of candidates in this era did not come about solely because of institutional reform. It also resulted from changes in popular attitudes. Prior to 1776, the public had been led to believe only the rich and well-born could properly fill governmental offices. The election literature of the time had stressed the idea that individuals lacking wealth and formal education were unfit for any posts. But, after independence, this pattern was in many cases reversed. The gentleman class was at times referred to as the "overgrown rich" and increasingly pictured as immoral and untrustworthy. In contrast, men without too much money and breeding were shown to be responsible and hard working, and thus more likely to serve the people well. "We know by frequent instances," declared one observer, "that the rich and high born are not the monopolizers of wisdom and virtue; on the contrary, these qualities are often to be found among the middling class in every country, who, being less dissipated and debauched than those who are usually called their betters, apply themselves with more industry . . . and in reality become better acquainted with the true interests of the society in which they live."[16] Of course, a representative was not supposed to be too poor; he had to possess enough property so as not to be tempted by bribes, and "yet not so much as to excite those little emotions of vanity in his bosom, which sometimes proceed from conscious opulence."[17]

In cities such as New York and Philadelphia the criticism of the wealthy was sometimes accompanied by calls for the election of artisans, who, it was claimed, were as capable of holding office as anyone else. "The respectable mechanics and carmen," one spokesman argued, "are not only adequate but entitled to the reins of government."[18] "Besides," injected another, "the smallest efforts of reason will tell you, may perhaps convince you, that the man who can build a shoe, or a pair of breeches in the best manner, so as to sit right and tight about you; that the man who can build with taste and judgment, so as to answer all the purposes and intents of a house, is the most likely person to build laws that will answer all ends and purposes of legislation. Therefore, let us have mechanics—and mechanics only for our legislators."[19]

Most campaign literature dealing with the candidate did not follow the above approach and rarely mentioned class or occupation. The writings on the subject focused primarily upon a man's moral characteristics. During the war years, patriotism was looked upon as the chief attribute a prospective official should possess. Voters in New Jersey were warned "not to intrust any one with the management of our public affairs who has not, by his vigilance and activity in the cause of liberty, proved himself to be a true friend of his country."[20] Naturally, patriotism alone was not sufficient. An office seeker was also supposed to exhibit such qualities as honesty, sagacity, and political expertise. As one essayist in New York exclaimed, "I think it the duty of every elector to lay aside all partiality and prejudice with regard to the external appearance of men, and choose only whom they know to be remarkable for true wisdom, integrity, an extensive political knowledge, fortitude of mind, and a uniform steadiness to the *American* cause."[21]

Following the war, many campaign tracts continued to urge voters to select honest and virtuous men with high moral standards.

"The great qualification of a legislator is *honesty*," professed a New Hampshirite, "and in the establishment of that, *a good character* is the great outline. The maxim, laid down by some writers, is a most dangerous one, that a bad man in private life may be a good man in a public capacity."[22] As political partisanship grew, electors were exhorted to shun demagogues, placeseekers, and especially "men of violent party spirit," who would "split the state into factions." "Choose honest, impartial, patriotic, and industrious men, who will pursue a middle line between the two parties," implored a Rhode Islander in 1787.[23] "If men of integrity, who had no interest distinct from that of the People at large were alone promoted to the legislature," insisted one Marylander, "this country would soon experience a degree of happiness hitherto unknown."[24]

Why men sought office during the Confederation era is not a simple question to answer. In the growing factional and issue-based politics of the times candidates were more apt to run in order to promote an interest or a particular cause. Some persons, having been elevated in status as a result of the war effort, perhaps wanted to become part of the decision-making process from which they had formerly been excluded. Others desired election because they thought it might lead to economic or professional gain. A few, like Alexander Hamilton, hoped for fame and glory. The majority, however, probably still served out of a sense of duty. Several men in this period stressed the idea of civic obligation when discussing the reason for ther participation in public life. James Warren of Massachusetts, for example, after being designated to sit in the legislature in 1787, told John Adams, "The dread of reviving the Clamour of refusing everything, joined with the Idea of its being the Duty of every Man to go upon Deck when called upon in a Storm, has Induced me to accept."[25]

As in the provincial era, many qualified persons refused to serve, usually citing personal and financial reasons. Edmund Randolph of Virginia said difficulties with his father's creditors prevented him from standing for election in 1783, rejecting James Madison's plea that legislative service was "a duty to which you owe some sacrifices." George Mason made no apologies, describing the attempt to send him to the Virginia House of Delegates in 1784 as "an oppressive & unjust Invasion of my personal Liberty."[26] At the same time, many individuals who agreed to serve remained for only a limited number of years, having no desire to continue for a long period. Of course, some short stays were the result of a man being ousted. In any event, the degree of turnover in the lower houses, though perhaps smaller than before 1776, was still considerable. By the late 1780s, it amounted to 46 percent in Virginia, 36 percent in New Jersey, and 32 percent in Rhode Island. In the latter state's seventy-seat assembly, only one man, William Bradford of Bristol, sat for all ten terms during the decade.[27]

Besides family hardship and loss of privacy, those interested in a public post faced other drawbacks. Although some improvements had been made in transportation, the journey to the capital continued to be a long and arduous one. Legislative sessions were more than ever taken up with endless meetings and tedious debates. Members of the house and senate, and even the chief executive in most states, still served without salary, receiving merely a small allotment for each day's attendance. Virginia provided ten shillings per day, Pennsylvania eight shillings and four pence, hardly enough to compensate a person for leaving his farm or business. For some individuals among the old line "Cosmopolitan" elite, the biggest drawback of all was the necessity of serving in a body dominated by men they considered narrow and provincial. Samuel Johnston, a high-ranking North Carolinian, expressed this feeling quite bluntly in 1784, saying: "I repent sincerely my having anything to do with the Assembly. I lose much more of myself than I gain to the public. The most illiberal dispositions prevail in most of the members."[28]

Whether it was because of the willing withdrawal of some dissatisfied gentlemen or because of the rejection of the same by a more politically aware citizenry, the kind of person being elected to the legislatures underwent tremendous change in the Revolutionary era. Prior to 1776, as Jackson T. Main has demonstrated, assemblymen were generally drawn from the upper levels of society. Upwards of 85 percent of the men chosen could be characterized as wealthy or well-to-do (owning two thousand pounds or more in property). A sizable percentage of this group consisted of large landowners or professionals—lawyers, doctors, merchants, etc. Furthermore, almost half of them came from prominent old families. Less than one in five, on the other hand, were men of moderate means—small farmers or artisans—with no distinguished family background.[29]

After the war, the composition of the legislatures proved to be very different. Men of wealth and established families were no longer so dominant. The proportion categorized as "wealthy" (owning over five thousand pounds) declined from 46 to 22 percent, and members from prominent old families fell from 40 to 16 percent. Large landholders and professionals were gradually replaced by those without much status. Undoubtedly many individuals who may be termed "well-to-do or better" continued to gain office, but as Main has emphasized, "their share decreased from four-fifths to just one-half."[30] The extent of change varied, of course, from one state to another, yet almost everywhere the trend was toward the election of more and more men of middle-class background.

The greatest transformation took place in New Hampshire. Those classified as wealthy or well-to-do had comprised 70 percent of the prewar assembly, but made up only 30 percent of the postwar body. Merchants and lawyers, formerly holding one-third of the seats, now possessed but one-tenth. Approximately 60 percent of the new assemblymen were yeoman farmers with moderate acreage. The alteration in New York's lower house was not as striking, though still considerable. Farmers, exclusive of large landowners, had provided 25 percent of the membership in 1769, but furnished 42 percent in 1785. The number of professionals, previously 57 percent, was cut in half. The yeoman-artisan middle class, which had contributed just half a dozen persons in the late provincial era, soon formed a majority. New Jersey's lower house membership was largely modified too. Three-fourths of the legislators elected in the earlier years were well-to-do; now two-thirds had only moderate wealth. Indeed, the typical house member in the 1760s held one thousand acres; the median in 1785 dipped to about three hundred acres. Around 66 percent of the new men were middling farmers, with merchants and lawyers retaining just six seats.

The Southern legislatures experienced a smaller shift. The strength of the great landowners in Virginia was reduced from 60 to 50 percent by 1785. Common farmers increased from 13 to 26 percent. Yet, the number of well-to-do, as opposed to wealthy, members saw a substantial rise. Median property ownership among delegates went down from 1,800 to 1,100 acres. Maryland's planter class representation dropped from 57 percent in 1765 to 36.5 percent in 1785. At the same time the proportion of farmers advanced from 18.5 percent to 28 percent. Altogether, delegates with moderate amounts of property, formerly holding one-fifth of the seats, now controlled one-third. In South Carolina, the percentage of wealthy representatives slipped from four-fifths to one-third by 1785. Merchants, lawyers, and doctors made up only 20 percent of the house compared with 36 percent twenty years earlier. Although most members were still well-to-do, the "Commons" was no longer the exclusively aristocratic body of pre-Revolutionary times.[31]

The change in the type of officeholder being elected was immediately evident to contemporaries from the moment of independence. Roger Atkinson of Virginia noticed that the newly chosen House of Burgesses in 1776 seemed to be "composed of men not quite so well dressed, nor so politely educated, nor so highly born as some Assemblies I have formerly seen. They are the People's men (and the People in general are right). They are plain and of consequence less disguised, but I believe to the full as honest, less intriguing, more sincere."[32] A Georgian, a few years later, saw the same thing happening in his state. The representatives, he said, were "taken from a class of citizens who hitherto have thought it more for their interest to be contented with a humbler walk in life."[33]

Not only were the less affluent more frequently designated; the same was true of men of non-English extraction. Prior to 1776, few persons of Scottish or German ancestry were ever chosen to hold office, even in states such as Pennsylvania where they comprised a considerable part of the population. Their loyalty and capability had constantly been brought into question. However, the patriotism and military prowess displayed by these peoples during the war made them more acceptable, and soon increasing numbers were being elected, especially from among the Scotch-Irish. By 1784, Benjamin Franklin claimed that in Pennsylvania "the Irish migrants and their children are now in possession of the government."[34] The Germans, while not providing as many representatives, produced certain key figures such as Frederick Muhlenberg, who eventually became speaker of the house in the first federal Congress.[35]

To be sure, extensive alteration in the kinds of men chosen to the legislature did not occur in every single state. In Rhode Island, it appears that very little change took place, at least before the mid-1780s. The great majority of the individuals gaining office continued to come from English backgrounds and from the highest economic ranks. While perhaps not as wealthy in absolute terms as prewar representatives, the new ones still came from the richest segments of the population. According to a study by Joel A. Cohen, 67 percent of the deputies were among the top 20 percent of the taxpayers in their respective towns, and 21 percent were from the next group. Thus, 88 percent of the assemblymen elected in the state between 1775 and 1784 were in the upper forty percent of their communities' property holders. Democracy in Rhode Island, he concludes, "was not a middle-class democracy."[36]

Professor Edward M. Cook has gone even further, questioning the whole concept of a "democratic" change in officeholding in the Revolutionary era. Many of the "new men" elevated to high office in this period, Cook admits, had not held important places prior to independence, nor had they been especially prominent in their native towns. But, he points out, the same could be said for a number of their predecessors a generation or two earlier. Frequently, the newcomers in major posts had been well established in the lower levels of the political hierarchy before 1776 and simply became logical candidates to fill the openings in the new state governments. The Gilmans and Pickerings of New Hampshire, he mentions, "were families that had belonged to the second level of the provincial elite for generations and were therefore prime candidates to fill positions left vacant by the fleeing Wentworths."[37]

Nevertheless, even Cook concedes that the system was actually changing. On the local as well as on the state level offices were becoming more political in nature. By the 1780s, men were increasingly elected on the basis of issues and factional attachments. In addition, because offices started to be more strictly defined and less flexible, voters did not feel the need to be so concerned with a candidate's wealth and personal background. Finally, the whole concept of deference toward the elite was declining. The hierarchical nature of provincial society, with its strict arrangements of rank and order, no longer had such a strong hold on the popular mind. "Political leaders," Cook concludes, "ceased being regarded as social superiors and became explicitly servants of the people."[38]

Thus, the Revolution fostered new attitudes and promoted changes in the qualifications for officeholders. This in turn brought forth new types of candidates and, by the end of the period, helped alter other phases of the officeholding system as well.

4

Nominations

The methods of nominating persons for elective office underwent a good deal of change during the Revolutionary era. The politicization of society had encouraged wider participation in the nomination process prior to independence, and this tendency was accelerated even further after 1776.[1] To be sure, nominations in many places remained the same as they had been in the provincial period: informal, simple, and personal, involving just the candidate and perhaps a few associates. But in more and more locales, organized, complex and broadly-based participatory patterns were gradually taking hold. By the end of the Confederation years in 1789, nominating procedures in several states already included a number of modern concepts.

The traditional uncomplicated forms of nomination continued primarily in the South and in those northern states where factionalism did not extend much beyond the legislature. Here, the basic means by which individuals signified their intention to run was self-announcement. This step was accomplished in various fashions. Prospective candidates would make some kind of declaration at a public gathering or write letters to prominent figures in the community informing them of their decision. Sometimes they would ask friends and relatives to spread the word about their availability. Colonel David Humphreys, former military aide to George Washington, told his brother, John, in Derby, Connecticut, in 1786, "I have no objections to its being known by my friends who are freemen of your town that I shall be on the spot, and if they should think proper to appoint me one of their representatives I will serve them as such—indeed you may show this letter where you think you can do it with discretion and propriety."[2]

In some of the towns and counties which published a newspaper, those desiring to stand for office increasingly made that fact known in the local press. A few weeks before the balloting the candidate would place a brief notice on the advertising page announcing his commitment. It contained no statement of his qualifications, merely a short and simple declaration of candidacy, with perhaps a request for support. For example, David Olden of Middlesex County, New Jersey, inserted the following in the *New Jersey Gazette* in the fall of 1782: "Having been solicited by many of my acquaintance, I intend to offer myself as a candidate for the sheriff's office at the ensuing election, where the favour of your votes will be gratefully acknowledged."[3] This approach was mostly used by those seeking administrative posts, such as sheriff and coroner, but some would-be legislators also adopted it.

By the late 1780s, candidates for statewide and national positions were beginning to announce their intentions in this manner too, though generally in a longer, more detailed letter. Cyrus Griffin, a delegate to the confederation Congress, declared in the *Virginia Independent Chronicle* that he would be "happy" to serve in the new House of Representatives. "Being at present in New York, he is ready to undertake the duties of employment, if the District shall think proper to confer upon him that honor."[4] Francis Corbin, a prominent planter, wishing to compete for the same spot, soon followed suit, noting that "several gentlemen in this district who have offered their services to represent it in Congress, have addressed our fellow-citizens by a PUBLIC LETTER. It has become necessary, therefore, for me to do so too."[5]

Open announcement of any kind was still unacceptable in many New England towns. As in earlier times, the inhabitants persisted in their belief that the office should seek the man. They frowned upon someone publicly declaring his candidacy or giving any outward hint of his availability. In the communities in which this view prevailed no formal nomination took place. On election day the citizens simply went to the ballot box and cast a vote for the person of their choice, who often had no idea he was being designated. This, of course, could lead to complications, for at times the man elected did not want to be in public life, and declined the post. Joseph Barrell, chosen as a representative in Boston in 1778, stated afterward: "How this matter came about I cannot conceive as I've made it my invaried rule to inform every person who mention'd it, that I could on no consideration think on serving."[6]

The practice of choosing a man without his knowledge was not confined to New England. In the South, where open nomination had always been more acceptable, individuals continued to be named to office without ever having been informed in advance. William Hooper of Hillsborough, North Carolina, after being selected to sit in the legislature in 1782, told a friend: "my election was altogether unsolicited and unexpected."[7] Two years earlier, William Hill from the town of Wilmington had the same experience. "The choice," he said, "was made without my Privity or Consent, and I knew not that any Person had set me up as a Candidate till near the close of the Poll."[8] In 1786, George Washington, attending the election of George Mason and Dr. David Stuart in Fairfax County, Virginia, noted that "the first [was chosen] contrary to, and after he had declared he could not serve . . . the other whilst he was absent in Richmond."[9]

In a number of districts, especially in the South, candidates were still being "set up" by an informal agreement among a small group of leading gentlemen. These men, usually planters in the rural areas or merchants and lawyers in the towns, would, after some consultation, pledge their support or "interest" to one particular individual or slate. Prominent figures in Orange County, Virginia, for instance, met in late 1787 and settled upon James Madison as the local standard-bearer for the state's constitutional ratifying convention. "It is the sincere Wish & desire of myself & a great many others," wrote neighboring planter Lawrence Taliaferro to Madison, then serving in Congress, "that you will . . . represent the People of this County in the Spring Convention & we Earnestly beg that you will be here some time before the election."[10]

Such arrangements as the one above were generally ad hoc and the designating group did not have much continuity from one election to the next. Though most Virginians seemed content with this system, a few raised some questions about the lack of regularity, claiming that it caused the choice of many unqualified persons for the legislature. They started calling for the establishment of periodic meetings at which they could nominate upstanding men of "clear and independent property."[11] However, there is little evidence that anyone took any steps towards this end in the years immediately following these pronouncements.

Candidates in the larger cities were commonly chosen by a more formalized nominating body known as a caucus. Although vague in origin, the caucus had been the chief mode of designating urban nominees since the early decades of the eighteenth century. At first exclusively the domain of gentlemen, the caucus gradually came to include many members of the artisan class. By 1776, tradesmen were exerting considerable influence in the caucuses of all the major capitals. Following the war, this influence expanded further, as artisans played a key role in the actual naming of candidates, rather than merely approving an already prepared list. In New York City and Philadelphia, the mechanics societies for a time created their own ticket, and even placed a few of their own kind on the slate. While well-to-do merchants and lawyers still controlled much of the urban political apparatus, tradesmen constituted an important element in the operation of the caucus and their contribution to the making of any ticket was deemed essential.[12]

Outside the cities, some groups began making nominations at county conventions. In certain states, such as Massachusetts, the county convention had developed originally for the purpose of dealing with various economic grievances, e.g., heavy taxes, lack of currency. Delegates picked by their towns would normally get together and issue resolutions aimed at bringing about desired policy changes. But at these meetings it became evident that perhaps a better way to alleviate adverse conditions was to back sympathetic candidates for high office. Therefore, at a countywide gathering in Worcester, in March, 1784, part of the proceedings was devoted to "who should be promoted to the principal offices in government."[13] Within a few years other counties in the Bay State were taking similar action.

The county conventions emerging in the Middle States never had any additional purpose other than the selection of candidates. They did, however, sometimes vary in form. At the outset, many of the meetings were essentially private get-togethers organized by a small clique or junto. One Pennsylvanian referred to them as "clandestine conventicles" comprised of about six, eight, or twelve self-appointed politicians.[14] But by the end of the war a growing number had been transformed into sizable groups of popularly-elected delegates. Under this system the electors in each township or district chose local representatives to a countywide gathering which ultimately decided on the nominees. In Kent County, Delaware, for example, deputies were selected from each "hundred" a few weeks before the regular contest. These men would then meet at Dover a short time later and designate the standard-bearers for each office to be filled.[15]

Meanwhile, several counties in Pennsylvania and New Jersey bypassed this method and began holding open meetings to nominate candidates directly. Such gatherings usually took place at a tavern or private residence with a fairly large body of people in attendance.[16] Whether the average citizen present could propose names or merely seconded a list previously drafted by county leaders is difficult to establish. Probably the latter was often the case. Nevertheless, the very fact that promoters of these meetings sometimes advertised them in the newspapers would seem to show a desire for popular input and support. The *New Jersey Gazette,* for example, carried the following in September, 1782: "Notice is given the freeholders and inhabitants of the county of Middlesex . . . to meet at the house of Thomas Nixon, in Cranberry, on Thursday the twelfth . . . then and there to meet and consult on proper persons to be chosen at the ensuing election, to represent the free citizens of said county in General Assembly."[17]

Some candidates in New Jersey and Pennsylvania were nominated by local militia units. As militiamen had frequently named their own officers, they merely extended their selection activities to include prospective legislators. Somerset County, New Jersey, formulated the most elaborate arrangement. Each of the militia companies in the eastern and western precincts appointed committees, which then met together and chose three men to stand for the lower house. Subsequently, a joint delegation would consult with emissaries from the northern precinct on the morning of election day in order to settle the final ticket. If a consensus was reached the eastern and western delegates might allow a substitute for one or two of their men; otherwise the original nominees would be supported. Militia groups in Monmouth and Burlington counties at this time appear to have taken part in similar negotiations to pick candidates.[18]

In Connecticut, nominations after 1776 continued in the unique manner that had developed there in the early colonial period. Each autumn the voters would designate twenty individuals to stand for the fourteen available spots (governor, deputy governor, and twelve assistants). The twenty men obtaining the highest totals were thus formally nominated and would run in the regular election held the following spring. Although this was theoretically an open primary with any freeholder eligible to be named, the whole process generated little enthusiasm at the polls, since the incumbent officeholders were ordinarily renominated. Changes traditionally came about only in cases of promotion, retirement, or death. Even when factional division set in, virtually no pre-nomination campaigning took place, and the printing of prepared tickets was almost completely unknown.[19]

There was one big exception within a brief period at the end of the war. In 1783, conflict over the impost, commutation of soldiers' pay, and a few other matters led Localist leaders to call a convention in Middletown. After taking a stand on the issues, the delegates published a special list of their own nominees for the twelve assistants' posts and had it widely distributed. Cosmopolitan opponents, seizing upon public dislike of factional activity, immediately sought to discredit the move. The open advocacy of a prearranged set of candidates was condemned as a "glaring impropriety" by a nationalist-minded critic. The nomination list made public by the Middletown Junto, he said, represented "a violation of the rights of the Freemen of the State."[20] The conventionites, declared another writer, would soon destroy the competency of the upper house, as they seemed determined "to drop every man of ability, of liberal and independent sentiments and in their room, to choose men of intrigue, who are artfully working upon the passions of the multitude to answer their own selfish purposes."[21] Such criticism may have been primarily partisan rhetoric. Nevertheless, this rhetoric was effective here, for none of the new men acquired enough votes to legally qualify. Yet, the next spring (1784), just before the regular election, the Middletown Convention reconvened and, disregarding many of the official designees, put forth their own slate of names. The list was subsequently printed in the *Norwich Packet,* though all six newcomers on it were sent down to defeat.[22] This proved to be the last effort of its kind. Despite continued division between Localist and Cosmopolitan elements, no further tickets or any evidence of electioneering prior to the fall nominations in Connecticut can be found.

During the late 1780s, as factionalism was increasing in most parts of the country, the nomination of high officials in certain states was undertaken by like-minded members of the legislature. Those involved—sometimes Localists, sometimes Cosmopolitans, and sometimes both—thought this practice would provide the public with guidance and enhance the election bid of their side's nominees. Such behind-the-scenes efforts did not go uncriticized. Just as the Middletown Junto's plan in Connecticut was attacked, so opponents would attempt to bring some of these subsequent schemes into disrepute, though usually to little avail. By the end of the decade several partisan legislative caucuses were either arranging their own slate of names or giving formal approval to candidates previously agreed upon by a few faction leaders.

In Virginia, where statewide factions were not fully operative until the debate over the Constitution, the initial legislative nominations occurred immediately preceding the election of the first federal Congress. Several Antifederalists in the Virginia Assembly in late 1788 drew up a list of ten candidates, which they circulated around the state. George Washington lamented the lack of such activity on the Federalist side. "It would seem to me, good policy," he wrote, for "the Federal Delegates (now in Assembly) of each district to confer freely together and resolve to support the fittest character therein; at any rate not to be disunited."[23] It is likely that this advice was heeded, at least in part, for Henry Lee later reported that in the northern districts, "it is probable that each party will fix on one man."[24]

Federalists in the Maryland legislature went further, not only choosing a complete congressional delegation, but publishing the list of names in the newspapers as well. "The following arrangement," the announcement began, "comes from a number of respectable Federal Characters in our Legislature, who are anxious to secure at this important Crisis, a GENUINE FEDERAL REPRESENTATION. Finding it impracticable to communicate with each District on the Subject, they have, from the best Information, put in nomination those Gentlemen who were believed to be most acceptable in their respective Districts."[25] The Antifederalists also published a congressional ticket, though whether it was prepared by a legislative group is not clear. The notice merely stated that "the nomination proceeds from a Number of Gentlemen who are jealous Guardians of the Rights of the People."[26]

The evolution of statewide nominating procedures in Rhode Island, Massachusetts, New York, and Pennsylvania—all having a greater degree of factional development—was more complex, often going beyond the legislative caucus. Since the new patterns that emerged in each of them are also better documented, they can be examined here in somewhat fuller detail.

Rhode Island had had a long tradition of partisan ticket-making going back to the provincial era. From the 1750s onward the Ward and Hopkins factions had both formulated tickets in private meetings shortly before the balloting. During the war years, with factionalism on the wane, the selection process devolved upon a small group of incumbent officials. As one writer declared, it had become "the Practice of the leading Men in this State, at the February Session of Assembly . . . to make what they call a Prox, containing the Nomination of the General Offices of Government for the Year.''[27] Sometimes the nominees then received formal approval at an open assemblage of interested electors, although how many attended such gatherings is impossible to tell.

In the late 1780s, when factionalism returned to the state, opposing groups again created separate tickets after holding lengthy secret negotiations. On occasion the competing slates contained some identical names, but in 1786 and 1787 the hard- and paper-money factions were so at odds with one another that they prepared two entirely different lists. The following letter from Samuel Ward of Newport (a supporter of longtime governor William Greene), to an associate, Welcome Arnold of Providence, in April, 1786, gives an excellent view of the political maneuvering that went on while the statewide ticket was being arranged for that year's election:

> I have not been at Newport since I saw you. I hear from undoubted authority that the gentlemen of that place are highly disgusted that the proposition respecting Mr. Mason was withdrawn, and the difference in proxing will be very great on that account. As it has always been my first wish that you should agree with Newp[or]t so now I give it as my ultimatum that the governors prox had best be printed with Mr. Masons name in the place of Mr. R____. I also take the liberty to advise that one or two gentlemen shall go from Providence to Newport on Sunday on which day the gentlemen of the court will be at home and agree upon that measure and upon some oppositions should they be judged necessary. I am decided that Col. C____ be opposed. I have taken the liberty to be very explicit to you—you know my attachment to your own person and to the Int[erest] of the state at large is unalterable. I think the harmonising you with Newport is the only chance of saving your prox. My wishes on that head do not arise so much from personal attachment to one person as from my apprehensions of something very wicked in a change. I think it is best to insist [on] Champlins Name in the Gov[ernors]

Prox. It stands in opposition—and that will make it impracticable to make use of mine. I presume the first three Delegates should stand as they are arranged in the opposition. General Lippert will make the fourth. I have wrote with so much freedom that I must instruct you to make no other use of this letter than to fully consider its contents without showing it and take measures your own judgment may suggest with my wishes that whatever they are they may be fortunate and happy.

I am
your sincere friend
S Ward[28]

Despite the seeming acceptance of private nominations by the end of the decade, the conservative minority in the legislature strongly condemned the pro-paper Country party's secret nominating procedures in the spring of 1789. "A Freeman," writing in the *Providence Gazette,* claimed that the choices for the gubernatorial ticket were concerted in a disreputable manner at a "nocturnal convention" in East Greenwich, after which everyone present was sworn to secrecy about what transpired. He tried to make it appear that such covert gatherings formed a new and improper mode of conducting the business. This system provided no popular input. No one, he said, "is to know who is held up for the public trust, and who is not till the moment he comes to town-meeting."[29] But it is clear that this was simply partisan rhetoric. Closed nomination meetings were already the established form used by both sides, and in the following years each would continue to hold secret conventions to arrange its slate.[30]

In Massachusetts, by the latter half of the 1780s, partisan nominating caucuses began to operate both inside and outside the legislature. These groups concentrated mainly on recommending candidates for the senate and the lieutenant-governorship. The first instance occurred in 1786 amid the state's deepening political and economic crisis and involved the conservative Bowdoin faction. According to a number of sources, several members had gathered at the end of the legislative session, "CAUCAUS'D it by counties, and agreed who should be elected Lt. Governour," and then approved a list of senatorial nominees for large and influential Suffolk County. The senate slate mentioned John Lowell, William Phillips, Cotton Tufts, and Stephen Metcalf as "certain"; General

William Heath, Jabez Fisher, and Richard Cranch as "doubtful."[31]
As in Rhode Island and Connecticut, the publication of a ticket was
quickly condemned as a scurrilous act. Opponents viewed the "new
mode" of open nomination as a gross "insult," for the servant was
dictating to the master "what he shall do." One essayist sarcastically
observed "how happy the Electors of the County of *Suffolk* must
esteem themselves, seeing *their Masters* have condescended to permit them to chuse *one* Senator at the next Election, *provided* they
confine themselves, however, either to *Judge Cranch* or *General
Heath.*"[32]

Prior to the choice of assemblymen in Boston the same year,
many different slates of candidates were prepared and the tickets
widely distributed. Although none of them was printed in the local
newspapers, one correspondent reported that "the secretaries to
the several CAUCUSES, have their hands full of business, writing
lists of Representatives." The author, continuing in the same vein
as previous critics, warned that the use of such lists ought to be
guarded against. The independent elector, he said, should know
beforehand the names of those he wishes to vote for, rather than
pin his "political faith on the sleeve of any interested party-
spirited caucuser whatever."[33]

The next year (1787) saw two further attempts at high-level nominating activity in the Bay State, this time by the so-called radical
side, but neither one was very successful. In the first, which followed Shays's Rebellion, officials of the town of Stoughton, still
sympathetic toward the Shaysite movement, suggested that a general
conference of Suffolk County delegates be held to select proper
candidates for the upper house. It was important for the "peace
and welfare" of the country that the "best men" be chosen senators, said the Stoughton selectmen, who called for a meeting at
Dedham where this could be arranged. Though the town of Dor-
chester approved, others rejected the idea, perhaps influenced by
articles in the *Massachusetts Centinel,* which denounced the pro-
posal as "seditious" and an "insult" to the state constitution.[34]

If the planned gathering in Suffolk County ultimately fell
through, a similar one set for Worcester County did take place. The
inhabitants of Lunenburg and Sutton appointed a committee to
write "Circular Letters" to all the towns in the vicinity, urging
them to send representatives to Worcester "in order to agree on
certain persons to be chosen as Governour, Lieut.-Governour, and
Senators for the ensuing year." Emissaries from several communi-

ties attended and it appears that a list of possible standard-bearers was handed about and deliberated upon. Yet no final agreement could be reached, and since many of those present seemed hesitant about making any binding decisions, the assemblage soon dissolved.[35]

No tickets were printed for the regular elections in 1787, but division over the choice of delegates to the state ratifying convention that December somehow signaled the start of widespread publication of candidate lists. At least six different slates of names to represent Boston eventually appeared in one or more of the city's newspapers. The winning ticket, according to Christopher Gore, was produced by a "junction of the North and South End caucuses," something that had not been achieved for many years.[36] While public nomination lists were still being condemned at this point, a few writers began to acknowledge their benefits. As one of them said, "it certainly gives opportunity for enquiry into and investigation of characters."[37]

Nomination lists in Massachusetts became even more prevalent at the time of the spring elections of 1788. Antifederalist senatorial tickets were distributed in several counties, including Worcester, Hampshire, and Bristol. Meanwhile, Federalists published a full slate of senatorial nominees for the entire state. "At a meeting of influential citizens from divers [parts of] the Commonwealth," a list of prospective senators had been worked out "with great care and circumspection," read the announcement.[38] Although it is difficult to say whether greater activity occurred before the first congressional contest the next winter, local party tickets for each side were again abundant. Thus, the ticket-making process in the Bay State had now become well established.

In New York, the presence of the British army in many parts of the state hindered the development of formalized nominating procedures during the war. Some groups held gatherings and issued tickets, yet this happened only on an irregular basis. But immediately after the British departure in 1783, periodic caucuses or county meetings were organized to choose legislative candidates, initially in New York City, and then elsewhere. Competing local interests dominated the early ticket-making efforts, though they soon became linked with the statewide factional struggle between the Clintonians and Anti-Clintonians.[39]

In each of the city's first few postwar elections several tickets were produced, most notably one by the organization of mechanics, who sought to elect a combination of artisans and middle-level merchants, and one by a more elitist group of wealthy merchants and lawyers. While both sides in 1783 placed a number of popular military figures on their ticket—John Lamb, Isaac Sears, Marius Willett, and William Malcolm—the mechanics' entry won by a large margin. The following year (1784), the mechanics, calling themselves "real whigs," put together a similar list, but the affluent merchant-lawyer clique, perhaps better organized, was victorious this time. In 1785, various competing tickets again appeared; some overlapping characterized the mechanics' slate and that of the "respectable Whig citizens," though the former turned out to be the more successful one.[40]

At about this time the preparation of competing tickets began to spread to other parts of the state. Albany witnessed its first publication of contending lists by the Clintonians and their Livingston-Schuyler adversaries in the 1785 election. A year later, in 1786, Clinton partisans also started printing tickets in Dutchess County, in spite of the charge that such practices were "contrary to all rules of modesty, of sound policy, and of wisdom." Then, in 1787, opposing lists surfaced in some additional counties, including Montgomery and Columbia. In the latter, delegates from several districts met at the town of Claverack and formed a county slate. But, as the Livingstons did not approve of all the selections, another meeting had to be held and a revised version put forth.[41]

The nominating process in New York became more formalized in 1788 as the two sides, now called Federalists and Antifederalists, each sought to capture a majority of seats in the state ratifying convention. The Federalists framed full party slates in a number of counties. In Albany, a committee of fifteen was appointed "to collect the sentiments of the different districts or townships of the county on the subject of nominating candidates." The Antifederalists went beyond this, organizing meetings in twelve of the thirteen counties, as representatives from the various districts in each one got together to select a single slate of nominees. In New York City, where the "Antis" were in the minority, they issued several lists, some of which contained the names of Federalists, hoping by means of this deception at least a few of their men would be chosen.[42]

A statewide nominating apparatus developed on an even larger basis for the gubernatorial election in early 1789. For the first time each party's candidate for the top post was publicly placed in nomination by a sizable caucus of sympathetic legislators. On February 3, George Clinton was unanimously renominated for the governorship by some forty of his Antifederalist supporters in the house and senate. Two weeks later, Robert Yates, after having been selected as Clinton's opponent by party leaders Alexander Hamilton and Philip Schuyler and approved by a large Federalist gathering in New York City, was formally nominated by a caucus of Federalist state senators in Albany. Subsequently, considerable numbers of "respectable freeholders" in many towns and counties around the state met together and designated either Clinton or Yates as their gubernatorial standard-bearer too.[43]

Pennsylvania probably experienced the greatest advancement in formalized nominating machinery of any state in the Confederation era. By the mid-1780s, if not earlier, open meetings to select candidates were being held regularly in Philadelphia, Cumberland, Montgomery, Northumberland, and perhaps several other counties. The county meeting in Northumberland was usually preceded first by discussions among faction leaders, and then by township meetings to choose delegates to the larger gathering. A letter from John Simpson of the Constitutionalist party to James Potter, a militia officer and prospective member of the assembly ticket in 1788, provides a glimpse of what transpired at the beginning of this process. "Your friends," he said, "has you in view for the House; [Samuel] Dale and Mr. Strawbridge are principally spoke of also. Your acceptance and approbation is requested to be early known. Next Saturday there is to be township meetings, to choose men to send to a county meeting the Wednesday following in order to form a general ticket. Before this time would wish to hear from you, for at that day you must be made known to the people, one way or other. To refuse it, I hope will not be the case."[44]

By the end of this period the most widely attended nomination meetings in the state, if not in the whole nation, took place in the city of Philadelphia. During the war the annual gatherings there had been small and secret, but, beginning in 1785, they expanded dramatically. The Constitutionalists, threatened by the rapidly emerging Republicans, started opening their proceedings to the public in hopes of achieving broader support. The Constitutionalist Society and its allies, the mechanics, formed a joint ticket, renaming the party's incumbent assemblymen as the standard-bearers.

The next year (1786), the Republicans, referring to themselves as "Friends of Equal Liberty," introduced public nominations too. They called their adherents to the Universal Baptist Meetinghouse to settle their ticket, one which subsequently scored an overwhelming victory.[45]

In 1787, widespread nomination activity prior to the assembly race in the City of Brotherly Love declined, at least on one side. The Constitutionalist party was rapidly losing strength, and if it held an open meeting there was no public mention of it. Yet, despite the dwindling opposition, the Republicans, or "Friends of the Federal Constitution," planned a huge gathering. According to all accounts, "a very great concourse of people attended the statehouse" on Saturday, October 6, and unanimously adopted a pro-Federalist slate. From the description in the newspapers it would appear that the large assemblage did not create the ticket, but did vote on each name selected in advance by the party hierarchy. It stated that "Mr. Nixon was chosen chairman, and Mr. Tench Coxe secretary of the meeting. Mr. Jackson having spoken, Mr. Gurney reported from a committee that had been previously appointed, the following names, William Will, Thomas Fitzsimons, George Clymer, Jacob Hiltzheimer, and William Lewis, which were separately offered to the consideration of the citizens present and approved of."[46]

The need to choose delegates to the constitutional ratifying convention in November of the same year led to an expansion of nominating activity in the state. Federalists and Antifederalists created competing tickets in Chester, Lancaster, York, and Berks counties. In Cumberland County, some leaders sought to form a single nonpartisan ticket. General John Armstrong, chairman of the meeting in Carlisle, pleaded with the people there to forget party attachments and "act as one man for the public good." But the committee named to designate the standard-bearers, consisting of representatives from each township, rejected Armstrong's advice and put together a slate that was completely Antifederalist.[47]

Antifederalists in the city of Philadelphia published a ticket with Benjamin Franklin's name at the top, hoping to draw some Federalist votes. This ploy had little impact and, as was the case for the previous assembly election, they did not hold any gathering to solicit public approval. The Federalists, on the other hand, organized a "very numerous meeting of the freemen at the statehouse," and agreed on Thomas McKean, James Wilson, Benjamin Rush,

Hilary Baker, and George Latimer as the party's standard-bearers. "The most remarkable unanimity appeared on the occasion," it was reported, with "not one name being offered to the meeting in opposition." Similar unanimity was achieved in Philadelphia County as a full Federalist slate was quickly nominated at a public house in Germantown.[48] These efforts helped assure Federalist success at the polls and ultimately at the convention.

Surely the most innovative development in the nomination process in Pennsylvania, or anywhere, materialized the following year (1788), prior to the election of the first federal Congress. Antifederalist leaders, unhappy with the new Constitution in its original form, sought to secure several amendments to it. Since favorable action on amendments could be accomplished only by a sympathetic Congress, these men began arranging for a statewide nominating convention to designate individuals who would pursue this goal. In July, when the Constitution had been ratified by ten states, party chieftains in Cumberland issued a circular letter to Antifederalists in each county proposing that representatives meet in Harrisburg to plan a course of action. The main order of business, besides formulating amendments, would be "to have proper persons put in nomination by the delegates in conference, [it] being the most likely method of directing the voices of electors to the same object and of obtaining the desired end."[49]

In response to the call, delegates from thirteen of the nineteen counties met in Harrisburg on the third of September. After a motion for a second constitutional convention was rejected and several amendments agreed upon, the body took up the subject of nominating prospective congressmen. At first the members considered creating an entire slate of Antifederalists, but many objected to this as not reflecting popular sentiment. Moreover, a majority probably felt that such a ticket would stand little chance of winning. Therefore, they adopted a compromise measure, and three Federalists, two of them Germans (Daniel Hiester and Peter Muhlenberg), were inserted onto a revised list.[50]

When the Federalists learned of the Harrisburg conference, they were outraged and severely criticized the secret methods used. One spokesman referred to the closed-door approach as "smuggling business." By what authority, he asked, did these men set themselves up to condemn the Constitution and form a congressional ticket for the express purpose of seeking amendments? In response, the Federalists began to hold a series of open county meetings "to take the sense of the people upon who should receive their franchises for representatives in Congress." At a gathering in Philadelphia, a committee consisting of leaders of the different wards was appointed to prepare a list of six suitable persons, any one of whom might be chosen a congressman. This body also selected two delegates to attend a party nominating convention in the town of Lancaster to take place in early November.[51]

Unlike the Antifederalist assemblage, which was convened for a number of purposes, the Federalist convention at Lancaster met solely to prepare a congressional slate. Delegates from eighteen counties appeared, five more than were represented at Harrisburg. In designating the eight prospective congressmen at large, they tried to represent the state on a broad geographical basis; but party affiliation remained the most important criterion. All the nominees eventually selected—George Clymer, Thomas Fitzsimons, Thomas Hartley, Frederick A. Muhlenberg, Thomas Scott, Henry Wyncoop, Samuel Chambers, and John Allison—were staunch Federalists.[52]

This development did not mark the end of the nomination process. Noting the presence of just two Germans on the Antifederal side, and of but one on the Federal side, several German spokesmen felt angered by this neglect. Pointing out that their group comprised one-third of Pennsylvania's population, they began demanding more representation. Subsequently, these individuals published tickets on both the Federal and Antifederal side, each containing all three previously-mentioned German names—Frederick A. Muhlenberg, Peter Muhlenberg, and Daniel Hiester. Altogether, many ticket variations were placed before the public prior to the balloting, and, as a result of the German community's efforts, the "German" Federalist slate ultimately triumphed.[53]

Thus, by the time the federal government was established in 1789, many new nomination procedures had developed. As statewide factions emerged, more systematic ways of selecting a ticket or standard-bearer became necessary in order to minimize internal division and maximize popular support. In some less politically organized regions the designation of candidates may still have continued in traditional ways such as self-announcement, but in those areas increasingly consumed by factionalism, more modern approaches—caucuses and conventions—were rapidly becoming the norm.

5

Electioneering

★★★★★★★★★★★★★★

The dimensions of electioneering stretched far beyond previous bounds during the Revolutionary era. Rising competition compelled office seekers to make much greater exertions to get elected. Quiet, low-key, gentlemanly methods of gaining favor, common in the past, gradually gave way to a more spirited and dynamic approach. New styles of campaigning were introduced, and old styles were intensified as the candidates and their followers broadened their appeal to win popular backing. If the pursuit of votes had been vigorous in a few instances prior to 1776, such efforts had tended to be the exception,[1] whereas less than a decade later in several states, they were becoming the rule.

Of course, compared to later epochs, many elections were still contested in a somewhat limited manner. A candidate in most states continued to run for public office on an individual basis, planning and executing the campaign himself aided perhaps by a few friends. Only in some of the more politically developed Middle States did sizable county organizations at times conduct a wide range of vote-getting activities. Numerous persons still stood for election on the strength of their personal attributes and achievements without any commitment to a particular party or issue. But regardless of one's connections or position in society it was not as easy to get elected as it had been in the past.

In earlier times, a member of the gentry rarely had to campaign much. He could even inject himself into a contest at the last moment and emerge victorious. But by the 1780s this was no longer true. Edmund Randolph of Virginia, who contemplated entering the assembly race in 1783, with the balloting just a few days away, quickly decided against it, saying: "The candidates having been active, and indefatigable, I might possibly expose myself to a mortification, were I to step forward at this late hour."[2] When former Attorney General of North Carolina James Iredell went ahead and declared his candidacy for the legislature one day preceding the election of 1787 he was easily defeated.[3] Even committing oneself to the field a week or two in advance was not usually sufficient unless it was accompanied by a diligent search for votes.

To be sure, it was still considered bad form in some states for a man to openly seek election. In Virginia and New England it had long been thought that the voter should make up his own mind when casting a ballot. Any attempt to influence an elector before the poll was seen as infringing upon his freedom of choice. In fact, certain constitutions made it illegal to interfere in the voting process through any form of bribery or force. Nevertheless, by the end of the Confederation period, the number of locales where candidates remained aloof was diminishing rapidly. Even the most staid New Englanders and courtly Virginians had come to realize that winning was often impossible without "stooping into the dirt" and begging for votes. General John Sullivan, for example, who had hoped to obtain the chief executive's spot in New Hampshire in 1785, but had "not taken a single step" to build a following, finished far behind his more zealous opponents in the final tally.[4]

Though it may have been increasingly necessary to solicit support, many gentlemen raised under the old system strongly disliked the task of open campaigning. They found it undignified, time-consuming, and harmful to friendships. Moreover, to engage in canvassing often meant compromising one's principles. Because of this some persons, like the conservative William Hooper of North Carolina, refused to partake in any such activities, preferring to suffer the consequences. As he told a friend before the legislative race in 1785: "It is a doubtful circumstance whether I shall be in the next Assembly. I have no desire to make any concessions to men whom I heartily despise, to secure their votes or interest."[5] Others, unwilling to accept defeat so easily, had to wrestle with their consciences over the proper course to take.

The dilemma facing a candidate hopeful of victory but reluctant to campaign was well expressed by James Madison on the eve of his struggle for a seat in the first Congress. "I am pressed much in several quarters," he said, "to try the effect of presence on the dis-

trict into which I fall, for electing a Representative; and am appre-
hensive that an omission of that expedient, may eventually expose
me to blame. At the same time I have an extreme distaste to steps
having an electioneering appearance, altho' they should lead to an
appointment in which I am disposed to serve the public; and am
very dubious moreover whether any step which might seem to
denote a solicitude on my part would not be as likely to operate
against as in favor of my pretensions."[6] Ultimately, Madison overcame his doubts and agreed to make electioneering appearances,
spending a number of weeks on the campaign trail.

Election campaigns after independence tended to be much longer
in duration than those of the provincial period. While some races
still lasted only a few days or a week, others proceeded for an entire
month or more. "Columbia County is five Weeks gone with Electioneering sickness," exclaimed Killian Van Rensselaer amid the
New York gubernatorial contest in 1789.[7] In those states consumed
by factional squabbles, each side's need to arrange many details
made it imperative that operations start early. The meetings of faction leaders to settle the ticket, the planning of overall strategy, the
distribution of ballots, the solicitation of support among the populace, and the preparation of items for the press all had to be organized well in advance of election day.

The atmosphere during a crucial campaign as well as some of the
actions taken by a party functionary are vividly described in a letter
from Judge Jasper Yeates of Lancaster, Pennsylvania, an Anti-
Constitutionalist, to his friend Colonel James Burd in October,
1778:

> I have been doing little for these ten days past, but elec-
> tioneering. Matters have come at length to that pass,
> that it becomes every good man to turn out, and endeav-
> or to procure a proper representation for the county he
> lives in. The many violations of the Constitution by the
> late Assembly have given the people at large the most
> general uneasiness and disgust, and strike the most
> ignorant with the propriety of an exertion at the ensuing
> election. A ticket has been formed here this day, which
> will run well in the district, and if there should be a divi-
> sion in other districts, [it] will probably be attended with
> success. Will not the people about Middletown vote? Be

good enough to try. We have written to Col. Cox on the subject, and enclosed him a ticket. Every moment's delay is attended with danger. In the city of Philadelphia and other counties, every nerve will be strained to effect a change of men and measures.[8]

Even in states less politically divided, local leaders sometimes had to make a multiplicity of arrangements. When strong competition was expected they followed a course very similar to that pursued in a heated statewide campaign. A letter from one of the faction heads to John Stevens in Hunterdon County, New Jersey, in 1784, traces the steps he and his associates had taken in the formative stages of that year's race. "We have had several Conferences on the subject previous to fixing the ticket," he explained, "& I have the pleasure to assure you, that the Inhabitants of Trenton Generally, as well as those of the lower part of the County, with whom we have had an opportunity of Conversing, are for the Ticket, & seem determined to push the Candidates with all their Interest . . . We are unwearied in our endeavours below, not doubting but that the good people of the middle & upper parts of the County, will heartily unite with us." A delegation was to "wait on Colonel Houghton in a few Days, & *if possible fix* him and his friends," in support of the ticket.[9]

Candidates and party managers, as the above examples illustrate, continued to seek the backing of prominent gentlemen in each community. Especially in statewide contests, it was very helpful to enlist the aid of such individuals, who could use their powers of persuasion upon the voters and upon other notable figures in the vicinity. During the ratification struggle in New York in 1788, Robert McClallen, a member of the Federalist committee in Albany, wrote to James Duane stressing the importance of having the tenants at Duanesburgh vote "right." He then asked Duane to use his influence with John Watts, Dirk Lefferts, Augustus Van Cortlandt, Augustus Van Horn, Peter Kissam, "and other Gentlemen who have any connections in this County," so that they too might pass on the proper word.[10]

Although eminent gentlemen were sought out for their support and interest, they themselves frequently used overseers, relatives, and family agents in direct dealings with the electors. This practice went on in many parts of the South, but was most common in the tenant-filled counties of upper New York. James Duane, for instance, employed his overseer, Abraham Oothout, to manage the campaign in Duanesburgh (Albany County) for the ratification contest, as well as at other times. Robert Livingston, on the upper manor in Dutchess County, had his sons "out attending the election" at nearby hamlets in 1788. "They had good success yesterday at Millers, today at Takkanick, tomorrow at Ancram," he told an acquaintance. A year earlier, the agent of the lower manor Livingstons planned to have the steward on Chancellor Livingston's mother's estate "go around in her name to the tenants a few days previous to the elections and request them to come out to vote."[11]

In the major towns and cities candidates were more likely to campaign in person, meeting with the inhabitants in various surroundings. Samuel Chase and David McMechen in Baltimore, for example, were known to mingle with the townspeople in taverns, and also marched with them in parades. Besides their playing an active role, urban candidates and their friends generally made a bigger quest for votes than did men elsewhere. They would often distribute handbills in the streets and place notices on bulletin boards, store fronts, and other buildings. Some party enthusiasts in Philadelphia went even further. According to one observer, "persons go from house to house, ransacking every story from cellar to garret, begging, praying and insisting on votes—and extorting promises of them." On election day itself, such individuals were known to stop people on the way to the polls, "forcing tickets into their hands."[12] In New York City, Antifederalists in 1788 prepared spurious ballots which "were dealt out as Federal Tickets with the Governor [Clinton] at the head, but so folded down as not to be perceived" by unsuspecting voters.[13]

During the heated Philadelphia election of 1785, Matthew Carey, publisher of the *Pennsylvania Evening Herald,* not only described the "barefaced exertions made in the streets" by the "partizans of both republicans and constitutionalists," but also recorded their actual conversations with the electors:

> Well, Tom, going to vote? . . . Yes? . . . My dear fellow, here's the staunch supporters of the constitution— your approved friends—men who have taken care of the mechanic's interest—huzza!—they are for the paper-money—Damn the bank—down with the bank for ever! —We'll have no nabobs—no great men—no *aristocrans* —huzza, boys! Success to the constitution for ever!—

My dear friends!—Happy to see you!—How are you,
Jack?—How's all your family, Bill?—What's the matter with you, Ned?—How do, Harry?—Welcome to
Philadelphia, once more, Dick.—Are you going to
vote?—Here's the ticket—friends of equal liberty—
men who understand trade and commerce—not the
damn'd prospeteran crew, who ride rough-shod over the
people, like Oliver Cromwell—huzza!—Three cheers!—
Commerce and equal liberty for ever!—Come on, my
lads, come on![14]

In the rural South, electioneering continued to function on a
more limited basis. Men who coveted a seat in the legislature in
Virginia and the Carolinas normally carried on their own campaigns, with only a few followers taking part. The candidate,
together with a companion, might travel about the district attending church meetings or militia trainings in order to gain support. A
former Pennsylvania military officer, Enos Reeves, visiting North
Carolina in 1782, told of a journey around Granville County in
which he accompanied Doctor Edward King, who was seeking election to the state senate. "To make interest for that purpose, I took
a ride with him among his friends in the upper part of the County.
. . . We [stopped] at what is call'd a Petty Muster, where the whole
was in his favour." The two men made several other appearances,
but King eventually lost the contest as his backers did not come to
the polls in sufficient numbers.[15]

Campaigns often reached a higher pitch in southern commercial
towns such as Edenton and Wilmington, North Carolina. Doctor
Hugh Williamson, later a delegate to the Constitutional Convention, told one correspondent that in Edenton, where he had decided
to run in 1785, "Electioneering was carry'd on with great Zeal. . . .
A couple of Gentlemen," he said, had "canvassed all the Town
over" for his opponents, spreading many "falsehoods." Archibald
Maclaine, a leader of the Cosmopolitan faction, mentioned "violence" and "chicane" as major elements in the Wilmington election of 1783, and prior to the contest there three years later warned
a friend that, in order to win, "everything depends upon mustering
all our forces, attending early, maturing our plans, and engaging
auxiliaries."[16] But if vigorous campaigning did occur in the urban
South on occasion, it did not usually spread very far.

Where the factional struggle and competition for votes were more severe, such as in Pennsylvania and Delaware, campaigns would at times be waged beyond a single district. On some occasions, Republican leaders in Pennsylvania would devise strategy for local races at centrally organized meetings. In 1786, General Anthony Wayne, upon returning to Chester County after consulting with party bigwigs in the capital, informed an associate: "I arrived from Philadelphia last evening. Our friends Morris, Clymer, Fitzsimons, etc. are exceedingly anxious about the Chester Election. . . . Frazer is the person who will be run by the Constitutionalists to a man—we must have no division in our ticket. Your People must make sacrifice of private prejudice to public utility."[17]

Increasingly, party chiefs sent agents from one county to another, providing money, printed matter, or political expertise in order to bolster their group's position in a tight race. During the heated legislative contest in Delaware in 1785, the Conservatives dispatched partisans from Kent County to Sussex to aid in the process of qualifying former Tories for the vote. Some emissaries could be extremely relentless in pursuing their cause. A certain magistrate supporting Samuel Lyman in his race against Theodore Sedgwick for the congressional seat in western Massachusetts in the spring of 1789 was said to have "pushed his horses so hard in pursuit of votes . . . that their marrow bones are visible at an immense distance—and it is much doubted whether said beasts will live to taste the herbage of the ensuing summer."[18]

Statewide competition of the governorship often required a more wide-ranging effort. In New York and the New England states, when such contests were expected, large numbers of people and resources would have to be summoned into the fray. In planning a gubernatorial campaign the candidate and his associates sometimes made a preliminary assessment of the popular support for their side. When wealthy Philip Schuyler of New York sought to replace George Clinton in the governor's chair either with himself or with John Jay in the mid-1780s, he sounded out opinions on this matter in almost every county.

In a rather lengthy letter to Jay, the former Revolutionary commander described the results of his survey. After mentioning his infirmities and his unwillingness to accept office even if elected, Schuyler urged Jay to run, insisting that he would ultimately defeat Clinton.

Those in this quarter [Albany County] will all decide for
you who would otherwise vote for me. In Ulster, Dutchess and Orange there will probably be such a diversity of
opinion as nearly to balance between you and Mr. Clinton. In Westchester we believe you will generally carry it
and so with Richmond. How Long Island will stand we
cannot form any opinion of. From New York we have
been privately sounded and it was justly observed that if
both you and I were held up both would fail, and I
afforded satisfaction in declining for reasons above
stated. As the party in the Metropolis who wish you is
respectable we have reason to believe that you would
have a very considerable majority there and from the
high estimation you stand in with all ranks it is not
improbable but that you would obtain almost all the
suffrages there.[19]

Even though Jay eventually refused to take part, Schuyler's account
illustrates the large amount of preparation that could go into
launching a gubernatorial campaign.

However much they operated behind the scenes, candidates for
the chief executive's spot in this era did not campaign publicly.
There is no record of any prospective governor canvassing, shaking
hands, or otherwise openly soliciting votes. Perhaps the fact that
four of the five elective governorships were in New England, where
overt electioneering was still somewhat frowned upon, explains this
lack of direct appeal. Nevertheless, a few governors, such as John
Hancock of Massachusetts and George Clinton of New York, did
try to cultivate an image as a "man of the people" during their
years in office. Moreover, these gentlemen often used patronage to
help maintain themselves in power, and Clinton, according to
Alexander Hamilton, was known to temporize on certain issues,
"especially when a new election approaches."[20] Yet seekers of the
high post basically left the procurement of votes to others.

By the late 1780s, some gubernatorial candidates in New England
began sending emissaries to visit various parts of their states. At
each stop these men would try to sound out public opinion and
drum up support for their favorite. The lawyer William Plumer,
after canvassing much of the interior of New Hampshire for General
John Sullivan in the winter of 1787, reported back: "In a late tour

through a very considerable number of towns on [the] Connecticut River, I was pleased to find, notwithstanding the many little and infamous tricks practised by the agents and tools of *certain characters,* that very many of the people, and many of the most respectable, were zealous advocates of your reelection."[21] Prior to the gubernatorial contest in Massachusetts between John Hancock and Elbridge Gerry in the spring of 1788, several Antifederalist leaders met at Dudley in Worcester County and "resolved to send messengers into every town in the counties of Worcester, Berkshire, Hampshire & Bristol & Middlesex, pointing the inhabitants of these places to Gerry & Warren for Govr. and Lt. Govr."[22]

Electioneering may have reached statewide proportions in some instances, but it did not usually go beyond that realm. The only interstate activity of any kind occurred in the selection of delegates to the various constitutional ratifying conventions in 1787–88. Although there was no national organization directing these efforts, party strategists on both sides sent messengers carrying campaign literature from one state to another, especially into New York, Virginia, and New Hampshire. The Antifederalist Committee in New York City, headed by John Lamb, also wrote letters containing strategy proposals to the Constitution's opponents in many areas—even as far away as South Carolina. Furthermore, essays on several aspects of the constitutional question in Philadelphia and New York City newspapers served as guides for editorialists all along the seaboard.[23]

Besides greater organization and expansion of the geographic bounds of campaigning, certain new means of gaining votes were introduced in these years. By the end of the period, candidates in some locales began appealing to the electorate through formal public speeches. Prior to the choosing of delegates to the state ratifying convention in New York in the spring of 1788, both Federalists and Antifederalists went around to speak at county meetings in search of support. A few months earlier in Baltimore, Samuel Chase, running for a seat in the legislature, addressed a "numerous and respectable body of citizens" at the courthouse on the shortcomings of the Constitution. Then, when seeking election to the Maryland ratifying convention from Anne Arundel County, Chase talked before sizable crowds in Annapolis and Elkridge, again taking a strong Antifederalist stand. This new method must have been effective, for it was soon reported in the press that "Anne Arundel county, though naturally Federal, have elected four Antifederalists, owing to the popular electioneering talents of Mr. Chase."[24]

In addition to prepared speeches, this era witnessed the first formal campaign debates between candidates. While vying for a spot in the Massachusetts ratifying convention in late 1787, Theodore Sedgwick of Stockbridge publicly discussed the contents of the new federal Constitution with his Antifederalist opponent John Bacon. According to Sedgwick, Bacon eventually became convinced by his arguments and wound up supporting the new document, though the latter vehemently denied it. Clearly the most celebrated series of pre-election exchanges pitted James Madison against James Monroe in Culpeper County, Virginia, amid the first congressional contest in the winter of 1789. After Madison's first solo appearance in the area, Monroe soon followed suit, in order to "erase any false impressions." Subsequently, the two men agreed to appear together to comment upon the Constitution and other matters. For two weeks they traveled about the county presenting their conflicting political views to the populace. Madison later described one of these encounters held before a gathering of German farmers whose votes were believed to be crucial. The meeting took place on a cold evening at a small Lutheran church. "Service was performed," he said, "and then they had music with two fiddles. . . . When it was over we addressed these people and kept them standing in the snow listening to the discussion of constitutional subjects. They stood it out very patiently—seemed to consider it a sort of fight [of] which they were required to be spectators. I then had to ride in the night twelve miles to quarters; and got my nose frostbitten, of which I bear the scar now."[25]

Along with the introduction of new forms of vote-getting came the enhancement of certain older forms, particularly that of treating the electors to food and drink. While the custom had already shifted from an impartial distribution of rewards to a means of securing votes well before 1776, it was now moving much further in that direction. In many places the candidates provided even more in the way of refreshment than their colonial forebears. Rum punch, wine, and beer were served in ever larger quantities, together with all sorts of additional fare. On election day in Washington County, Maryland, in January, 1789, the local Federalists prepared a lavish feast near the courthouse. "An ox roasted whole, hoof and horn, was divided into morsels, and every one would taste a bit," declared an onlooker. The people, he added, "were so happy to get a piece of Federal Ox as ever superstitious Christians or Anti-Christians were to get relics from Jerusalem."[26]

The practice of treating flourished despite a growing belief in its impropriety, stricter laws against abuses, and regular contests at short intervals. As Edmund Pendleton, longtime leader of the lower house of Virginia, lamented in 1785:

> I had hoped that our annual elections would have put a stop to every Species of bribery, and Restored perfect freedom in the choice of our representatives in General Assembly, but am sorry to find myself disappointed. In a neighbouring County (as I am told) three Candidates have emploied as many Months in canvassing not only from house to house, but at frequent and expensive treats; a species of bribery the more dangerous, since it is masqued, and appears not in its plain shape as a piece of offered gold would. In our County, a new declaring Candidate at the last Court, made a sacrifice of much wine, bottles and glass to the fortunate Deities.[27]

One possible exception to the seemingly heavier use of treats was the state of New York, where the Beekmans and Livingstons had once spent a good deal of money to set up tables covered with beef, bread, and brew. According to the historian Alfred F. Young, extensive treating was gradually being replaced by more coercive means of acquiring votes, especially on the part of landlords with their tenants. After the Revolution, he asserts, "there is less evidence of hand shaking and treating and more evidence of threats to collect overdue rents or to enforce fines for the alienation of property."[28] Yet one contemporary politician, Abraham Yates, claimed that in counties experiencing vigorous competition among the gentry, earlier forms persisted. "The public houses in every quarter were opened and a trial made [as to] who had the most influence and the largest purse."[29]

Although treating still prevailed, some of the tricky and deceptive vote-getting techniques from the provincial era had disappeared. The records show few, if any, cases of transferring land to the landless just prior to election day (creating so-called fagot votes), of candidates agreeing to serve without pay or offering their stipend to charity, of choosing fewer men than the number of spots available on the ticket, or the outright buying of votes with cash. More stringent laws and better enforcement undoubtedly contributed to the elimination of such nefarious methods. Furthermore, many persons had come to believe that corrupt forms of electioneering had no place in the politics of the new "virtuous" republic.

Naturally, not all unscrupulous activity ceased at this time. One questionable practice from the earlier period continued to flourish, perhaps to a greater degree than before: the spreading of false rumors. In quite a few contests during the 1780s factional spokesmen deliberately distorted an adversary's political affiliation or his view on a particular issue. For example, amid the competition for places in the New York ratifying convention, opponents claimed John Jay sided with the Antifederalists when he was actually a Federalist. Virginians attempting to stop James Madison's bid for a seat in the first Congress unfairly charged that he had spoken against any amendments to the Constitution.[30] Such accusations proved difficult to refute, though in the instances mentioned both Jay and Madison were successful.

A similar type of subterfuge was an announcement that a certain gentleman had withdrawn from the race or was unwilling to serve. James Bowdoin, leading gubernatorial aspirant in Massachusetts in 1785, had to overcome several such devious statements in order to be elected. On at least one occasion, schemers used the contrary approach. That is, a man who had openly declared he was not running was held up as a bona fide candidate in the hope of deceiving the voters. In the 1789 congressional campaign in Middlesex County, Massachusetts, Antifederalist supporters of Elbridge Gerry tried to make the electors believe that Nathaniel Gorham was in the race in order to reduce the vote for the real Federalist standard-bearer, William Hull. This ploy proved successful, as Gerry was subsequently chosen.[31]

Another underhanded means of electioneering which developed further in this era was the "gerrymander," though not yet known by this name. While unequal election districts had been created in colonial times, none were drawn in such an extremely partisan manner as were a few of those for the first congressional contests in New York and Virginia. Antifederalists in the New York legislature, when arranging boundaries, sought to consolidate their strongholds and to isolate Federalist areas. But their deceitful strategy failed to achieve the desired results, as Federalists won an equal number of seats in the balloting. The most notorious effort along these lines was the brainchild of Patrick Henry and his friends in the Virginia legislature aimed at keeping James Madison out of the U.S. House of Representatives. They formed a weirdly-shaped district, placing Madison's Orange County with others that were strongly Antifederal. Nevertheless, Henry's manipulations did not work out as planned, for Madison, through heavy campaigning, was able to thwart the design and obtain victory.[32]

Easily the most significant development in electioneering during this era was the expanded use of the press. In the few weeks before an election, the public prints often carried numerous essays related to the contest; some also offered lists of candidates for the people to consider. By 1789, about ninety separate newspapers were in circulation, almost twice the number in 1775, many of them tri-weeklies and dailies. Newspapers now operated not only in large cities such as Boston, New York, and Philadelphia, but in smaller urban centers like Worcester, Massachusetts, Poughkeepsie, New York, and Carlisle, Pennsylvania as well. Several small southern towns such as Fredericksburg, Petersburg, and Winchester, Virginia, and New Bern, North Carolina, had begun publishing newspapers on a regular basis, too.[33]

Besides enlarging their pre-election coverage, newspapers of this period started printing much more frankly partisan material. Many contributors began taking sides, no longer simply calling for the election of "good men." Increasingly, they extolled the alleged virtues of one candidate and brutally attacked the supposed short-comings of his opponent, finding it most advantageous to empha-size the latter phase. Even in Massachusetts, where personal assaults had long been considered improper, malicious statements about those running for office soon became widespread. As Van Beck Hall has written about press campaigns in the Bay State in these years:

> Every contested election for one of the state's higher offices uncovered character assassins who blackened the reputation of every leading politician within the state. Bowdoin was portrayed as a Tory or a trimmer, as the leader of an aristocratic junto, or as a nepotist. Hancock was pilloried as immoral, incompetent, lazy,

stupid, a secret Tory sympathizer, and as a poor busi-
nessman. Samuel Adams was execrated as a public
embezzler, the enemy of George Washington, and a
crusty autocrat. Thomas Cushing was pictured as a
creature of Hancock, a nepotist and a weakling. Benjamin Lincoln was shown to be another aristocrat, a mili-
tarist, and an admirer of monarchy. The highpoint of
abuse, Stephen Higginson's "Letters of Laco," a vitri-
olic denunciation of Hancock, merely went a trifle further than similar defamations of character during the
decade.[34]

Eventually newspapers went beyond carrying a few partisan
items, and started to reflect a distinct political point of view. By the
late 1780s, a number of major sheets, such as the *Independent
Gazetteer* in Philadelphia and the *Massachusetts Centinel* in
Boston, were firmly in the Antifederalist or Federalist camp.
Although not official party organs, they served much the same purpose. Thus, even before the newspaper war in the years of the first
party system in the 1790s, a politically active and partisan press was
developing. Despite some complaints, newspaper appeals for votes
had become more or less common. The *Centinel* in a sense had
legitimized this process as early as 1785, when it began to place the
heading "Electioneering" at the top of columns devoted to campaign material.[35]

In addition to newspapers, political pamphlets continued to be a
valuable vote-getting tool. Pamphlets most often contained extended versions of newspaper essays, though sometimes they were completely original works. A majority of them stressed one key issue
such as paper money, regulation of commerce, or treatment of
Loyalists. The post-Revolutionary tracts tended to be written in
plainer language than earlier ones so that they could be read and
absorbed by the average freeman. When Tench Coxe of Pennsylvania prepared a paper for the inhabitants of the western counties on
the subject of representation, he told a friend, "Tis a simple style,
calculated to be understood, where education blesses but few and in
a small degree."[36] While not as influential as newspapers, pamphlets, especially those published at the time of ratification, probably
had a considerable impact on the outcome of many races.

Broadsides or handbills were still widely used, too, primarily in towns and cities. They would usually be handed out in the streets or posted on buildings shortly before election day. Most such sheets consisted of brief statements about the candidates or about a particular issue. For example, in 1783, several broadsides were printed at the time of the legislative race in New York City; one called for the designation of men with political experience, another emphasized the need to elect "mechanics," a third warned against the choice of those who would pardon Tories. Prior to the contests in Baltimore and Annapolis in 1786 and 1787, a few broadsides advocated support for individuals favoring paper money. As was true of other forms of printed matter, the largest number of broadsides appeared during the election of delegates to the state ratifying conventions in 1787-88.[37]

Whether in broadsides, pamphlets, or newspaper articles, the candidates and their associates increasingly appealed to voters on an ethnic or religious basis. In the states containing a heterogeneous population, faction leaders recognized the importance of ethnic and religious ties and the need to gain the support of certain groups. For instance, Pennsylvania propagandists constantly urged the large German element to vote as a bloc in order to protect their standing. Baltimore politicians in 1788 called upon the Irish to favor James McHenry because of his Celtic ancestry. Samuel Chase, McHenry's adversary, retaliated with a broadside entitled "To the Roman Catholic Voters," claiming that he could better serve their interests. The conservative faction in Delaware sought to attract the Episcopalian vote by denouncing its opponents as violent Presbyterians. The West Jersey Junto used a similar ploy to gain Quaker backing in the congressional race in early 1789. "Come Friend, go to the Election and vote for the West Jersey ticket, the Quakers ticket," one sheet began. "Come, turn out, oppose the Prysbeterian Ticket. The Prysbeterians want another War. . . . [If] You don't feel a Freedom [to vote], you will lose your freedom, Your Liberty and Your Property, nay more, Your Religion."[38]

Beyond ethnic and religious appeals, there was also a rise in electioneering on the basis of class, mainly in certain cities. As early as the summer of 1776 the Radical party in Philadelphia urged voters "to chuse no rich men and [as] few learned men [as] possible to represent them in the [state constitutional] convention."[39] In New York City, after 1783, several newspaper essays specifically urged the election of mechanics. "The pedantic lawyer, the wealthy merchant, and the lordly landholder, have already had their interests sufficiently attended to," insisted one of them.[40] While some statements of this type may have legitimately represented the views of their authors, many others were just partisan attempts by crafty politicians out to gain working-class support. Most brazen in their efforts were the affluent Samuel Chase and his associates in Baltimore, who frequently portrayed themselves as friends of the poor, and their Federalist opponents as tyrannical aristocrats. Chase constantly charged that the business community was using economic coercion upon the common people, threatening not to employ mechanics unless they voted "as the great men please."[41]

Perhaps the state where the new electioneering methods became most fully operative was Maryland. From the year 1786 onward one can observe in every campaign a very sophisticated use of the press, with appeals being made to voters on the basis of social class and religious and ethnic background. Articles often included forecasts of doom. Antifederalists warned that the new Constitution would lead to higher taxes, monopolies, military conscription, and religious persecution. They even asserted that Prince William Henry, the third son of George III, might become king of America. Besides the press, Maryland politicians began to seek votes through public speeches and rallies. Finally, they introduced the idea of attracting wide-scale attention by holding elaborate parades. On the day of the assembly contest in Baltimore in 1788, Federalists marched along the main streets of the city in support of their two candidates, James McHenry and John Coulter. Behind them, gangs of sailors carried a ship and pilot boat, all within a spirited atmosphere of drums beating, fifes playing, and colors flying.[42]

The increasingly vigorous electioneering efforts of the Confederation era eventually brought forth many critical comments about their nature. While most were the work of disgruntled partisans, some reflected an honest belief that free and open elections, and, by implication, the American system of government, stood in imminent danger of destruction. Although such negative statements had appeared once in a while during the colonial period, they became much more frequent and angry in tone a decade after independence. A Philadelphian in 1786 asked, "Through what mud and dirt will not the tools and runners of party wade, and what horrid meanness will they not stoop to answer and serve the vile purposes of party and faction?"[43] A New Hampshirite condemned those "who wish to bribe our votes by emissaries, handshakes, and holiday sociabilities, and those who address us with the more silent, but not less sophistical artifice of newspaper panegyric."[44]

Some critics saw the new campaigning practices reflecting a decline in American virtue and a yielding to corrupt British patterns. A correspondent for the *Massachusetts Spy* in 1785 claimed that the "scurrility" that disgraced the recent gubernatorial contest resulted from "too closely copying that part of British manners which does not add dignity to government."[45] A few years later a Virginian complained that the way candidates in his state begged and threatened voters was "exactly similar to the Election of the corrupt and infamous House of Commons."[46] Yet Jonathan Jackson of Newburyport, Massachusetts, felt that Americans had gone beyond the English in this respect. When the spreading of false rumors hurt his congressional campaign in 1789, Jackson declared: "Let us not any more reproach Great Britain for their practices; they are more open and manly."[47]

Regardless of whether or not these judgments were true, it is clear that electioneering during the Revolutionary period had proceeded in a modern direction. While the quest for votes had occasionally been strenuous in the years before 1776 and would become much more so after 1790, the intervening era provided an important bridge. Candidates were going to much greater lengths to get elected, introducing a profusion of new methods to garner additional votes. The gentlemanly approach used in previous times was definitely on the wane, and would never return.

6

Voting Procedures

★ ★ ★ ★ ★ ★ ★ ★ ★ ★ ★ ★ ★ ★

The termination of royal authority in 1776 led to many changes in the voting process itself. Various arbitrary methods, once in standard use, now began to be removed. The officials in charge were put under much stricter surveillance. New American practices, more democratic in nature, gradually replaced long-standing British ones.[1] Several states, in their constitutions and subsequent laws, introduced measures to regularize elections, equalize representation, and make polling places better accessible. Over the course of the Revolutionary period the whole apparatus was altered in multitudinous ways to assure greater participation and popular control.

One of the most disturbing features of the voting system under British rule had been the irregularity and infrequency of elections in many locales. Elections in the eight royal colonies and proprietary Maryland had been called at the discretion of the governor, sometimes within a few months, but sometimes not for a number of years. While triennial and septennial acts had normally forced chief executives to schedule a poll within a certain length of time, they did not provide a sufficient limitation. Such long terms between contests (three to seven years) had often made legislators less dependent upon their constituents and more easily dominated by crown and proprietary influences.

To try to remedy the situation, Patriot leaders proposed the adoption of regular elections at short intervals. "If rulers knew that they shall, in a short term of time, be again out of power, and . . . liable to be called [to] account for misconduct," declared one spokesman, "it will guard them against maladministration."[2] This plan quickly received widespread support and it was implemented in numerous state constitutions. Elaborating upon its importance some framers stressed the concept of "a frequent recurrence to fundamental principles," which implied the need for representatives to go back to the people periodically for renewed authority. After noting that elections should be held often, the North Carolina declaration of rights stated that a "frequent recurrence to fundamental principles is absolutely necessary to preserve the blessings of liberty."

Although the idea of fixed and shorter terms was generally agreed upon, the determination of the exact time limit or rate of frequency aroused a good deal of controversy. Some conservatives, such as Carter Braxton of Virginia, argued that triennial elections would be frequent enough, but most contemporaries believed that only annual elections would furnish proper safeguards. As John Adams asserted in his influential essay *Thoughts on Government* (1776), there did not exist "in the whole circle of the sciences a maxim more infallible than this, 'where annual elections end, there slavery begins.' " These words soon became a rallying cry for many Whigs, including Samuel Adams and Thomas Jefferson. Consequently, all the states which formed new constitutions, except South Carolina, made provision for a yearly selection of the lower house.[3]

Several states instituted frequent election of higher officials too. The new popularly-elected governors in both Massachusetts and New Hampshire were to be designated annually, joining the chief executives in Connecticut and Rhode Island, who were already chosen in that manner. New York, the other state to introduce gubernatorial elections to the citizenry, did so on a three-year basis. Similarly, the upper houses of the new legislatures were in most cases to be selected at relatively short intervals. Six states—Massachusetts, New Hampshire, Connecticut, Rhode Island, New Jersey, and North Carolina—now had annual elections of the upper chamber. South Carolina scheduled contests every two years, Delaware every three years, New York and Virginia after four years. Maryland's senate, which was picked by members of an electoral college, sat for the longest term—five years.[4]

The inauguration of regular, short-term elections brought with it the creation of specific times on the calendar instead of arbitrary ones for the actual balloting. Thus, many states now had a permanently established month and day to begin polling. According to its new constitution, Massachusetts was to designate its major officers on the first Monday in April. New York laws stipulated that the event take place on the last Tuesday in April. Maryland assigned the first Monday in October for its selection process, and Pennsylvania and New Jersey named the second Tuesday of that month. Virginia, while not setting an exact date, directed that representatives be chosen "in the month of April in every year, on the court days of each respective county or corporation." The occasion for assembly voting in New England towns continued to be dictated by the local selectmen. Their options, however, were relatively limited, since the contest had to occur a few weeks before the initial spring meeting of the General Court.[5]

Another key development was the rise in the number of individual elections, which resulted from the extension of representation westward. Following independence, people in many formerly unrepresented frontier areas and recently incorporated towns could for the first time vote and send delegates to the legislature. By 1789, Pennsylvanians were electing representatives in nineteen counties instead of eleven. North Carolinians were choosing men from over sixty counties and towns, compared to forty-three a decade and a half earlier. Dozens of new townships in Massachusetts and New Hampshire started holding contests, and older ones which had not previously designated deputies now began to do so. Within a short time, the lower house in New Hampshire had expanded from 34 to over 80 members, that of Massachusetts from 110 to about 350.[6]

Even where very few new counties or townships were formed, the number of representatives per voting unit often increased. After 1776, New Jersey counties elected three delegates rather than two, and Delaware enlarged its county slates from six to seven. In South Carolina, the amount per rural parish tripled from two to six in many cases, while St. Philip's and St. Michael's parishes (Charleston), which formerly combined to choose seven, began selecting a total of thirty. Despite the latter state's small size, its assembly was now the second largest, encompassing some 202 members. As one South Carolinian explained: "An ample Representation in every Republick, constitutes the most powerful Protection of Freedom, the strongest Bulwark against the Attacks of Despotism," since corruption—"that almost invincible Assailant of the best formed Constitutions"—could never arrive at "such irresistible Strength in a *full* as in a *nearly empty* House."[7]

More important than the gain in delegates per unit was the attempt in several states to equalize representation itself. The colonists had long lived under a system where counties of one thousand inhabitants often chose as many assemblymen as those with over two thousand. When Revolutionary leaders criticized the lack of representation in Parliament, some groups of Americans began calling for an end to such inequities at home. Anxious to maintain broad popular support, numerous states seriously considered these demands. Although Virginia, Maryland, and North Carolina kept their system of uniform county representation regardless of size, others, such as Pennsylvania, New York, Georgia, and South Carolina, took steps to reapportion their legislatures according to population or the number of taxpayers. As the authors of the Pennsylvania Constitution of 1776 put it, "Representation in proportion to the number of taxable inhabitants is the only principle which can at all times secure liberty and make the voice of a majority of people the law of the land."[8]

While the aims of this movement were not fully achieved (partly from design and partly because of inadequate census data), legislative seats in the four above mentioned states did become more equitably distributed by the end of the era. Pennsylvania first reapportioned its lower house in 1779 and did so again in 1786. The overrepresented older counties of Bucks and Chester found themselves reduced from eight delegates to four, whereas newer and larger Lancaster and York, having previously designated six between them, now voted for six apiece. The New York Assembly, which had generally allotted two members to every county, adjusted the number upward on a proportional basis, populous Ulster and Dutchess receiving six and seven, respectively. The state of Georgia gradually introduced proportional representation too. Under its constitution of 1777, there were to be ten members for each county, with the exception of Liberty, which contained three parishes and was allowed fourteen. Then, a revision in 1789 gave proportionately larger representation to all deserving counties. South Carolina, though not establishing equal representation, did give the backcountry area many more seats than it had had before, and stipulated in its constitution of 1778 that reapportionment would occur every fourteen years.[9]

Massachusetts also made some progress toward equalization. Prior to 1776, any town with a few hundred settlers was entitled to send one deputy to the General Court, though the city of Boston, with a population of over fifteen thousand, could choose only four. When the new state constitution was being prepared, several Bostonians and inhabitants of other large communities complained that wealth and numbers ought to be taken into account in determining representation. As a result, the constitution of 1780, while retaining the township as the basic unit, gave considerable weight to population. Incorporated towns with 150 rateable polls (i.e., freemen above sixteen years of age) were allowed one representative, towns with 375 rateable polls two representatives, and towns with 600 rateable polls three representatives, plus another one for each additional 225 rateable polls.[10]

New Hampshire followed a similar pattern. Its constitution held to the concept of town representation but based the number of delegates on the total "rateable male polls, of twenty-one years of age and upwards." Each town with 150 rateable polls was granted one representative; any with 450 polls was permitted two representatives, with an extra one given for each additional 300 polls. Communities containing fewer than 150 polls could be grouped together in order to qualify for representation. Within a short time, the latter method became the one most frequently practiced. Merely a third of the towns had their own separate house member, and only Portsmouth (four) and Amherst (two) possessed more than one.

Neither Rhode Island nor Connecticut made any adjustments in their long-standing systems of town representation, so that their lower houses simply became further malapportioned. As Rhode Island was still operating under its charter of 1663, Providence elected the same number of deputies as Warwick and Portsmouth (four), though it had grown to be twice as populous as the former and four times as populous as the latter. Expanding mainland locales such as South Kingstown and Gloucester also had inadequate representation. Meanwhile, Connecticut continued to adhere to its charter provision of 1662, calling for an assembly with a membership "not exceeding two Persons from each Place, Town, or City." Thus, its large towns, such as New Haven and Hartford, were similarly underrepresented. Not until the nineteenth century did either state introduce any significant modifications.[11]

Equitable representation was applied in even fewer cases in the election of the upper houses or senates. The assistants in Connecticut and Rhode Island continued to be selected on a statewide basis along with the governor. In New Jersey, Delaware, Pennsylvania, and North Carolina, councillors or senators were designated on a county basis—one per county—with no concern for population size. Virginia created twenty-four senatorial districts, though without much consideration for population, either. However, Massachusetts, New Hampshire, and New York all introduced some form of proportional representation. Under the new provisions, Massachusetts elected forty senators in thirteen districts, six men each in populous Suffolk and Essex; New Hampshire picked twelve senators in five districts, with five from Rockingham County; New York chose twenty-four senators in four districts (nine in the southern region—New York City and the surrounding area), and agreed that in the future reapportionment would take place if a septennial census showed it to be necessary.[12]

In every state, the initial step in the calling of an election remained the governor's issuance of a writ addressed to the local officials in charge of the proceedings. It directed them to summon all the eligible voters in the district to meet at a specified time in a particular spot in order to choose men to fill certain offices. The types of individuals qualified to vote, whether freemen, freeholders, or taxpayers, were usually more carefully spelled out to avoid some of the confusion that occurred at times in the provincial period.

Upon setting the date, the officials were generally compelled by law to give the populace a good deal of advance warning about the impending election. North Carolina required a minimum of twenty days, New Hampshire fifteen days, and Massachusetts ten days, though Pennsylvania and New York, having regularly established dates, permitted as little as eight days for the posting of the announcement. With the majority of states setting up and advertising standard dates, it was becoming less possible for partisan officials to deceive the public by failing to give proper notice.[13]

Nevertheless, in parts of New England, voters in a number of cases contended that they had not been informed of the event. In New Hampshire, at least six petitions were presented to the assembly between 1778 and 1786 complaining about this type of impropriety. The first incident followed the designation of representatives at New Durham Gore in 1778, when several protesters insisted that "the Inhabitants of the gore had no Kind of notice or warning that there was to be such a choice."[14] Massachusetts witnessed many more such occurrences. According to the study by David Syrett, numerous instances of irregularity can be found in the process of summoning people to election meetings. He points out that not one town in Lincoln County was represented in the legislature in 1779 until the last part of the session "because the sheriff received the precepts after the date of election, and the General Court had to reissue them before the election could be held." In addition, he claims that fraudulent methods were sometimes used in calling town meetings "to assure that the votes cast would be subsequently ruled illegal." Not until the year 1787 did the Bay State attempt to penalize those guilty of improper conduct in these matters.[15]

News of an impending election continued to be made known to the public in the same general fashion as before. In North Carolina, the sheriff was required to post a proclamation "at the courthouse and other public places in the county." New York officials were called upon to give notices "by writing" in "at least three of the most public places" in the district. The constables in Pennsylvania were supposed to provide notice in six different spots. Local officers in New England informed the townspeople by tacking the announcement on the meetinghouse door, though at times they used other locations. For example, in Lee, Massachusetts, in March, 1780, they "Voted to Warn the Town Meetings by Setting up Notifications in four Deferant Places Near at Peter Willocks house and Amos Manfield Mill and Ashbal Lee Grismill and John Winegar Grismill."[16]

In the larger cities from Boston to Savannah, newspapers gradually became the primary means of publicizing upcoming elections. The following notice in a Charleston, South Carolina, newspaper in November, 1788, is typical:

> By virtue of a Writ of Election to us directed, Notice is hereby given, To such persons as are qualified to vote for Representatives of the General Assembly, that an election for the purpose of choosing one suitable person, to serve in Congress, and two Senators for this state, and thirty Members for the General Assembly of the same, will be held at the parish church of St. Michael, Charleston, on Monday and Tuesday, the 24th and 25th days of November, from the hours of 9 to 12 in the morning, and from two to four in the afternoon of each respective day.[17]

One of the major voting innovations in certain states was the increase in the number of polling places. Outside of New England towns, most men prior to 1776 had to travel to the county seat to cast their ballot, sometimes covering a distance of ten to twenty-five miles. This situation still prevailed in parts of the South such as Virginia and Maryland. But under the new election laws in the Middle States such long journeys to the polls were no longer necessary. Responding to the pleas of those having difficulty reaching the single voting site, New York and New Jersey soon designated specific townships and other places where tickets could be delivered, while Pennsylvania divided its existing counties into several voting districts.

The New York legislature perhaps went the furthest in this sphere, enacting a law in 1778 which stated that all future elections should be held "not by counties but by boroughs, towns, manors, districts, and precincts." A decade later, Abraham Yates noted that returns had come in from eight polling places in Columbia County and eleven in Albany County.[18] New Jersey went almost as far. Only thirteen polling spots existed at the time of independence, one for each county. However, in 1779 the legislature permitted the creation of extra voting sites in Essex, Hunterdon, and Sussex. Each ensuing election law in the 1780s saw more counties being given additional locations. By 1788, the polls could be adjourned to specified towns in every county. The total number of places where one could vote had now reached fifty-three, over four times the original figure.[19] Pennsylvania eventually achieved a similar result, separating its counties into voting districts beginning with the choice of delegates to its constitutional convention in 1776. This concept was sanctified by law in 1777, and forty districts were formed within the eleven counties. In 1785, the number of individual units expanded to fifty-two; York was now split into five parts, Lancaster and Chester into four each.[20]

The rise in the number of voting districts soon led to the establishment of some new kinds of polling places. The county courthouse, practically the only location where voting had occurred in the middle colonies, now became just one of several sites. Taverns emerged as the most popular alternative in New Jersey. Mills and schoolhouses as well as taverns were frequently employed in Pennsylvania. Elsewhere, the types of polling places did not change very much. Throughout New England, voters still cast their ballots at the town meetinghouse. Virginians and North Carolinians continued to use the county courthouse. In South Carolina, the parish church remained the traditional spot, though in a few districts the courthouse or a private residence was assigned. Georgia held its elections in churches, courthouses, and individuals' homes, as it had done in the past.[21]

The number of voting days for any contest continued to vary. In New England, where people voted on a township basis and distances were short, balloting was still confined to a single day. One day also remained the standard in Pennsylvania. The polls in North and South Carolina generally stayed open two days, unless the candidates agreed to close them sooner. Maryland and Virginia allowed voting to go on for up to four days, and New York for as many as five days, at the discretion of the presiding officials. New Jersey had no statutory limitation, and while most encounters ended within a few days, there was one exception. Partisans in Gloucester and Burlington counties during the first congressional election in early 1789 kept the ballot boxes open for more than three weeks, and Essex County leaders did so for almost ten weeks![22]

Most states still did not specify the exact hours the polls should be open, and apparently left the decision on such matters to the men in charge. The officials in each New England town set their own time span; Portsmouth, New Hampshire, for example, allowed voting from 10 A.M. to 5 P.M. A few states, however, did have uniform regulations. New York stipulated that votes be taken from one hour after sunrise until sunset, and Georgia ordered that balloting proceed from 9 A.M. to 6 P.M. Pennsylvania announced that the polls should open between ten in the morning and two in the afternoon and be shut down at seven in the evening, except in Philadelphia, where the deadline was extended one hour. But many workingmen in the City of Brotherly Love believed it should be extended even further. Finally, in 1786, the assembly altered the closing provision to permit every elector present at the statehouse by eight o'clock to cast his vote.[23]

Because of the increased number of polling places and the creation of specific voting dates, the weather became less of a factor in keeping men away from the ballot box. Most statewide elections were scheduled for the spring (in Virginia, New York and the New England states) or early fall (in Maryland, Delaware, Pennsylvania, and New Jersey). Only in the milder climate of South Carolina and Georgia did the voters choose legislators and other officials in late

November or early December. A few instances of low turnout or postponement due to inclement weather did occur at local New England elections held in the month of March. At the Plymouth, Massachusetts, town meeting of March 25, 1776, "the Weather being Cold and but five people Appeared Therefore the Meeting was Adjourned to Monday."[24] The weather also had an effect upon some contests that were not part of the regular pattern, such as the designation of representatives to the first federal Congress in the winter of 1788-89. Correspondents from several counties in Pennsylvania reported that chilling frosts and other bad conditions had severely limited attendance.[25]

Overall, elections after 1776 seem to have been more somber and serious events than those of the late provincial period. The festive atmosphere once associated with election day was no longer so prevalent. Post-election celebrations were often curtailed. The removal of royal government brought an end to much of the pomp and ceremony connected with contests in each capital. Upon watching what transpired in Boston in 1780, the lawyer William Pynchon remarked, "Well! This is the day for election of Governor, Senate, etc., according to the new Constitution; but at noon no cannon is heard, no 42 pounders as formerly on Election days."[26] The actual casting of ballots was usually carried on in a more orderly fashion, too. Tumults, petty brawls, and other disruptions common in the previous era now decreased in number.

Yet in some locales election day still meant a time of great excitement and ceaseless activity, frequently accompanied by widespread disorder. After the vote was taken in Sussex County, Virginia, in April, 1788, much fighting occurred, the participants striking one another with "fists and cudgels."[27] At the contest in the North Carolina town of Edenton three years earlier, several men had to employ their "Toledo trusty of stubborn Hickory" to keep peace at the poll.[28] Assessing voting conditions in New York City in the late 1780s, Samuel Blachley Webb declared, " 'Tis all confusion— parties for different sides appear publicly—and sometimes blows ensue." Webb, a former army officer, claimed that on one occasion he was "so beat and bruised" he had to be "confined to his room for four days."[29]

Even greater turbulence occurred during and shortly after the war in parts of New Jersey, Pennsylvania, and Delaware, where Whig-Tory divisions were especially sharp. Probably the most violent outbursts took place in Delaware's Kent and Sussex counties, hotbeds of Toryism. In 1783, the ballot box in Kent was removed by an armed band of British sympathizers, while in Sussex, a number of soldiers "with swords, bayonets and clubs" terrified the electors, "beating and abusing several persons." Four years later, numerous Sussex voters were attacked by "an armed body of about two hundred Men," resulting in many severe injuries. Elsewhere, by this time, such high feelings and bloodshed had gradually given way to more orderliness and tranquillity. In Burlington, New Jersey, once known for heavy strife, an observer at the scene in 1788 stated that "the business was conducted in a manner that did honor to freemen exercising one of their highest privileges."[30]

At the polling place, the entire proceedings were generally overseen by a staff of several officials. In New England, these continued to be headed by the town selectmen or town meeting moderator; in South Carolina, the parish church wardens officiated; while in most other southern states, the sheriff was still in charge. New York and New Jersey, wishing to limit the power formerly displayed by sheriffs, replaced them with a set of locally elected judges and inspectors. Proponents of the change in these two states thought that popular control of the election machinery would reduce partisanship and conflict. Nevertheless, it seems that the new method did not work out well as far as New Jersey was concerned, for the faction in command often filled the positions with men who favored its candidates.[31]

The sheriff, wherever he was in charge, continued to exert enormous influence upon the outcome of a contest. He could still open and close the polls at his own volition, choose his own clerks to record the ballots, judge the qualifications of electors, and, in certain states such as North Carolina, cast the deciding vote in case of a tie. Yet it would appear from the records that sheriffs no longer acted in as arbitrary a manner as they did during the provincial period. On the whole, citizens registered far fewer complaints about high-handed sheriffs violating the rules. Undoubtedly the removal of royal government and the threat of heavy penalties were the factors most responsible for the decline. The state of Virginia, for example, had established a fine of one hundred pounds for any breach of duty by the sheriff, and other states called for nearly as large a sum.[32]

Election day festivities usually began with a statement by the official in charge, who recited the procedures to be observed and the types of posts to be filled. In some places the church bells would be rung or a town crier sent around to signal the start of the event. The election inspectors in New York were required to read the following proclamation three times in a loud voice: "Hear ye, hear ye, hear ye, the poll of this election is opened, and all manner of persons attending the same, are strictly charged and commanded by the authority, and in the name of the people of this State, to keep the peace thereof, during their attendance at this election, upon pain of imprisonment."[33] After completion of these preliminaries, the voting would commence.

Methods of balloting continued to differ according to place. Voting was still done by the spoken word in Virginia, Maryland, and parts of other states. Carrying on a tradition inherited from England through their colonial ancestors, the electors here would gather at the county courthouse and, if the outcome was at all in doubt, would line up to deliver their vote orally. When the polls opened, each person would enter the courthouse and come up to a long table staffed by the sheriff and his clerks. Then, after swearing that he was duly qualified, the voter would call out the names of the men he wished to have chosen. Frequently, the candidates themselves would be in attendance and publicly thank the man who had just voted for them. A clerk would subsequently record the voter's name in the appropriate columns of a large poll sheet situated in front of him. The polling would go on in this manner until it appeared that all of the votes were in or it became time to shut down the polls for the day. In Virginia, just before terminating the proceedings, the sheriff would call out, "Gentlemen Freeholders, come into court, and give your votes, or the poll will be closed."[34] Following this announcement, the last names would be entered and a final tally made.

Although open voting remained acceptable in Virginia and Maryland, many reformers in the Middle States started clamoring for change. Since the early 1770s they had strongly asserted that the *viva voce* method placed undue pressure upon the elector, especially where tenant farmers were forced to vote in the presence of their landlord. Proponents claimed the introduction of paper balloting would prevent "Men of Property, Power, and Tyrannical dispositions from prostituting their Wealth and Influence."[35] Influenced by such arguments, certain states such as New York and New Jersey began making the shift from oral voting to the paper ballot. Balloting by paper, it is true, was already well known in New England, Pennsylvania, Delaware, and the Carolinas in the period of British rule. But after independence it became the only form acceptable in these locales.

The biggest conversion took place in New York. The framers of its new constitution (1777) announced that "whereas an opinion hath long prevailed among diverse good people of this state, that voting at elections by ballot would tend more to preserve the liberty and freedom of the people, than voting *viva voce*," a "fair experiment" with paper balloting should be made. Henceforth, though senators and assemblymen would continue to be designated in the traditional fashion, the governor and lieutenant governor were to be elected by written ballot. It was also specified that after the war the legislature be given authority to abolish voice voting altogether if the new alternative proved effective. By 1787 it would appear that the trial had been favorable, for the new election law passed that year stipulated that all voting was to be conducted by written ballot thereafter.[36]

In New Jersey, paper balloting was adopted on a more gradual and piecemeal basis. Beginning with the election to the provincial congress in May, 1775, Somerset County introduced written ballots. Subsequently, the comprehensive election law of 1777 established voting by ballot in seven of the thirteen counties. No explanation for this division was given, but apparently the law allowed each county full autonomy in its choice of methods. Several counties switched back and forth in the next few years; the election law of 1782, for instance, shows only five counties using the ballot. Yet by 1788 at least nine of the counties had embraced the written form, and the rest would soon follow.[37]

Pennsylvania provides a good example of the movement away from a mixed system toward a single system of paper balloting. Prior to 1776, men who arrived at the polls without ballots were permitted to give their votes orally. For illiterate voters, it was required that the sheriff read them the names on their tickets to make sure that those were indeed the desired choices. If not, they too could give their votes orally. In 1777, however, the legislature declared that "it is highly dangerous to the freedom of elections in this commonwealth that the sheriffs and other persons appointed judges . . . should continue to be invested with the power of searching and discovering for whom any elector shall vote," and stated that thereafter no ticket should be opened, and that no one should be allowed to cast a voice vote. A short time later, ballots were required to be folded before being deposited, which in effect made them secret.[38]

The New England states in the years after independence still saw a few elections decided by means other than the paper ballot. Local officials in some towns were occasionally chosen by a show of hands. At the assembly contest in Salem, Massachusetts, in 1776, "the Electors voted by Kernels of Corn and Pease." The town of Mendon, when passing judgment on the proposed state constitution of 1778, had "those members of the meeting who approve the Constitution . . . repair to the west end of the Meeting House, and those who do not . . . move to the east end of the meeting house."[39] But these were exceptions; after 1776, almost all voting in the Bay State, as well as in New Hampshire, Connecticut, and Rhode Island, was carried on by paper ballot.

The ballots used in most of New England consisted of plain pieces of paper on which the townsman entered the names of his choices. Rhode Island, however, continued to have its competing factions prepare an elaborate ticket containing an entire slate of candidates, sometimes with a partisan slogan at the top. These were not secret ballots, but items printed in bulk and widely distributed throughout the state. In either case, people voted by simply dropping the slip of paper or printed ticket into a hat or ballot box. Massachusetts, which chose its governor, lieutenant governor, and senators on separate slips, had three different boxes. The depositories were usually set down at the front of the meetinghouse near a table where the moderator or selectmen sat. These officials would watch the proceedings carefully to see that only qualified citizens participated and that nobody inserted more than one sheet of paper.[40]

Voting procedures tended to be fairly similar in other states using written ballots. In Georgia paper slips were to be taken "by two or more justices of the peace . . . who shall provide a convenient box for receiving said ballots." In North Carolina, two boxes were set up, one for senatorial ballots, the other for representatives. After a man filled out his two tickets, he was required to have each one "rolled up, & dropped, in presence of the Sheriff & Inspector, into the box, thro' a small hole made for the purpose." Electors in Pennsylvania and New Jersey normally wrote down their own preferences, but in some counties faction leaders handed out prepared tickets. Though a fine was supposed to be levied against anyone who gave an illiterate person a ticket with names other than those he requested, the ignorant were frequently deceived. "Tickets are often palmed upon such as cannot write or read," declared William Paterson of New Jersey, "by which means they sometimes vote *in* the person whom they intended to vote *out*."[41]

There appear to have been few, if any, changes in the methods of counting and certifying ballots. The North Carolina law stated that "when the election shall be finished the returning officers & inspectors shall open the boxes and take out Tickets and call over the names therein inserted, and number the ballots." The poll lists in New York were to be tallied and, following "due examination and correction" by the inspectors, certified and delivered to the county sheriff. In Pennsylvania, the judges and inspectors in each district had to count the votes and prepare a "fair list" of the totals for each candidate. Then, within two days, the judges were required to meet at the county seat and, after comparing the figures from the different districts, "certify and declare those who bear the highest number of votes to be duly elected."[42]

The number of disputed elections seems to have diminished during the years after independence. Certain states, most notably Virginia and Maryland, which had previously experienced numerous protests, now faced significantly fewer of them. Perhaps a reduction in competition at times as well as an easing of voter qualifications can in part account for the decline. Also, as noted earlier, election officials were less apt to engage in fraudulent behavior. But such nefarious activity by no means disappeared. In fact, several instances of fraud in the taking and counting of votes were recorded in this era. The Lancaster County, Pennsylvania, elections in 1778 and 1784 both involved charges of stuffing the ballot boxes. At the contest in New Bern, North Carolina, between William Blount and Richard Dobbs Straight in 1779, the "Tin Canister without a Top" used as the depository was allegedly left unsealed and unguarded, allowing many illegal ballots to be dropped in. Even Boston was not exempt from corrupt activities, the results in 1782 showing more votes than voters. When this happened, the town selectmen ordered that in the future "no Votes would be received but such as are unfolded," and "all those persons who Vote for Representatives shall on their giving in their respective Votes, enter into the Hall and there remaine, untill the Poll is closed."[43]

In the event of fraud or other wrongful action, a defeated candidate had the opportunity to lodge a formal protest with the legislature. The lower house had long held the privilege of judging its own membership, and thereby assumed the right to resolve disputed elections. In some states the entire body or an ad hoc group would hear the complaint, though the southern states usually had a standing committee on elections to review the proceedings. The members would go about their work most diligently, examining poll lists and interrogating witnesses before reaching a final decision. The plaintiff's appeal was sustained on occasion, but in the majority of cases the previous outcome was affirmed and the petitioner's plea rejected. Generally, small infractions of the rules were overlooked, as the legislature showed little enthusiasm for voiding the original result, especially if the candidate himself was not at fault.[44]

As in the provincial period, the proportion of votes necessary for a candidate to be elected—plurality or majority—was not always well defined in the statutes. Yet, from looking at the available results, it seems that, outside New England, only a simple plurality was needed. On the other hand, Connecticut, Massachusetts, and New Hampshire clearly required a full majority. When no individual obtained a majority in the latter states' gubernatorial contests the winner had to be designated by the legislature. This happened once in Massachusetts, three times in New Hampshire, and five times in Connecticut during the 1780s. The situation became even more complicated in the choice of representatives to the first Congress in 1788-89, as the verdict in many cases was determined by run-off elections. It took three ballotings in New Hampshire and three to five in some districts of Massachusetts before every race was decided.[45]

After the votes were tabulated and lists of the results prepared and certified, the returns had to be made to the legislature within a specified period of time. Twenty days was the limit in Virginia, seventeen days in Massachusetts, and just twelve days in Pennsylvania. Most returns were made on time, but in Massachusetts it would appear that several towns did not comply, for there were numerous blank spaces in the official totals each year. Eventually, in 1787, a stronger law was passed compelling the selectmen and county sheriffs to dispatch the returns within the given span of time. (Virginia and Pennsylvania had previously enacted such laws.) When the notice of the outcome was finally received and certified by the legislature, the winning candidates would then be officially elected.[46]

Thus, by the end of the Revolutionary era, voting procedures had been substantially reformed. Many arbitrary practices had been eliminated. Elections had become more regular and frequent, representation in the legislature more just and equitable, polling places more numerous and accessible, and balloting more orderly and secret. While a few states still clung to some of their old ways, which limited popular participation and control, the majority of them had moved in a more democratic direction.

7

Turnout

★★★★★★★★★★★★★

Voter turnout in Revolutionary America was rather small during the early war years but grew considerably after that time. Extensive figures from seven states—Massachusetts, Connecticut, New Hampshire, Rhode Island, New York, Pennsylvania, and Maryland —plus scattered data from the other six reveal that only about 10 to 15 percent of the adult white males took part in contests held between 1776 and 1779. Yet by the late 1780s more than twice that number (perhaps 20 to 30 percent) were regularly coming to the polls. Moreover, if the calculations were made on the basis of eligible voters, the percentage would have been even higher. At least five states had occasions where upwards of 40 percent of the qualified electors delivered a vote.[1]

Attendance had generally fallen off at the beginning of the 1770s as a result of growing patriot unity, and it slipped even further once independence was declared and the fighting commenced. Substantial turnout became impossible under wartime conditions. Loyalist sympathizers were barred, soldiers had to leave home, and some people found themselves cut off from the ballot box or in British-occupied areas. But with the cessation of hostilities in the early 1780s the size of the vote started to increase. Regular elections were restored everywhere. Troops returned from service, often thoroughly politicized. Factionalism resumed in several states and new issues such as paper money emerged. Also, the removal of test laws, better access to the polls, and other procedural changes made it easier to cast a ballot. Indeed, many men were exercising their suffrage rights for the first time, which added significantly to the number of participants.

By the end of the Confederation era it would appear that voting totals in a majority of states ordinarily surpassed prewar figures. Although data are often fragmentary it seems that the turnout in New Hampshire, Massachusetts, New Jersey, Pennsylvania, Delaware, Maryland, and North Carolina was generally higher than before. It is even possible that this was true for South Carolina and Georgia. On the other hand, Connecticut and Rhode Island never reached the sizable tallies of the late 1760s until the end of the century. In addition, Virginia's output dropped off substantially in the decade after independence and so did New York's. Nevertheless, voter participation was on the rise in more states than it was on the decline. In fact, in numerous cases bigger aggregates were produced in the latter half of the 1780s than in the 1790s, when national parties began operating. The Massachusetts election returns for 1787 exceeded any obtained there until 1800. The New Hampshire gubernatorial vote from 1785 to 1789 usually stood ten percentage points above that registered in the subsequent decade. Even in states like Maryland, in which turnout became larger in the Federal period, the rate of growth in the ten years preceding 1789 was greater than in the same time span following that date.[2]

From the seven states where fairly abundant figures exist for the 1780s, we find New Hampshire having achieved the highest turnout, with 30 to 45 percent of its adult males balloting in each year's governor's race. Rhode Island averaged only 20 percent, but, on the basis of qualified voters, was closer to 30 percent for its gubernatorial contests. Pennsylvania and Maryland, electing just legislators and county officials, saw roughly 20 to 35 percent coming to the polls. Connecticut, Massachusetts, and New York, experiencing less competition, had a voting rate of only 15 percent, though in the latter two it did reach twice that on important occasions. Data found for the other states are too limited to generalize from, though it would appear that Delaware and New Jersey amassed quite respectable totals in certain instances.

The following is a survey of the available information about turnout in each of the original thirteen states, 1776–89.

NEW HAMPSHIRE

New Hampshire had the highest percentage returns of any state, at least after yearly gubernatorial elections were inaugurated under its new constitution in 1784. In the six contests for statewide office staged between 1784 and 1789, the turnout averaged more than 37 percent of the adult white males, and on two occasions it rose above 43 percent (see table 1). The lofty figures can be attributed partly to the heated personal rivalry in most governorship races and partly to the fact that balloting took place at the annual town meeting in March, when all local officials were chosen as well.

The first gubernatorial election (1784) attracted the smallest number of voters of the six under consideration. Only about 5,000

TABLE 1

**New Hampshire Gubernatorial Elections,
1784–1789**

	Number of Votes	Percentage of Adult White Males		Number of Votes	Percentage of Adult White Males
1784			**1787**		
M. Weare	c. 3,500		J. Langdon	4,034	
G. Atkinson	c. 500		J. Sullivan	3,642[a]	
Scattered	c. 1,000		J. Bartlett	628	
	c. 5,000	30.0	S. Livermore	603	
			Scattered	378	
1785				9,285	43.1
G. Atkinson	2,755				
J. Langdon	2,497[a]		**1788**		
J. Sullivan	777		J. Langdon	4,421	
J. Bartlett	720		J. Sullivan	3,366	
Scattered	330		Scattered	1,053	36.9
	7,079	37.1		8,840	
1786			**1789**		
J. Sullivan	4,309		J. Sullivan	3,657[a]	
J. Langdon	3,600		J. Pickering	3,488	
Scattered	658		J. Bartlett	968	
	8,567	44.9	Scattered	421	
				8,534	32.3

[a] Chosen to the governorship by the legislature

men (30 percent) cast ballots as longtime political leader Meshech Weare ran virtually unopposed. Weare received approximately two-thirds of the total, his nearest adversary, George Atkinson, getting just 10 percent. After Weare's retirement the following year the struggle for the chief executive's spot intensified. Several candidates actively competed, and many more people came to the polls. Some 7,079 votes (37.1 percent) were delivered in 1785, with Atkinson acquiring 2,755 and John Langdon 2,497. As neither man had obtained a majority the legislature was given the choice and made Langdon the winner. In 1786, 8,567 (44.9 percent) voted, the largest percentage turnout of all, with former Revolutionary war general John Sullivan defeating John Langdon in a hard-fought race, 4,309 to 3,600. The next year (1787), 9,285 persons (43.1 percent) took part, as Langdon outscored Sullivan this time, 4,034 to 3,642. Langdon, however, did not secure a popular majority, and the legislature returned the more widely-known Sullivan to office. In 1788, with 8,840 (36.9 percent) participating, Langdon did gain a full majority, but barely so, having one more vote (4,421) than the amount needed. Sullivan on this occasion managed just 3,366. Fewer votes were recorded in the election of 1789, when Langdon was no longer a candidate. Although the aggregate of 8,534 was only about 300 less than the previous one, the percentage (32.3) went down by four and a half points. John Sullivan was restored to the governor's post once again, garnering 3,657 votes compared to 3,488 for his closest challenger, the lawyer John Pickering.

There is hardly any information about the designation of members to the state ratifying convention, though totals for this event were probably small. The contests to choose congressmen and presidential Electors in mid-December, 1788, for which exact counts are known produced higher figures than in most other states yet lower than for any New Hampshire gubernatorial encounter. Only 5,126 ballots (21.4 percent) were cast for those seeking to be federal representatives, and 4,028 (16.8 percent) for the prospective presidential Electors. As no candidate came up with a majority in the congressional race, a run-off had to be held the following February. In this second election 2,776 (11.6 percent) voted, little more than half that registered in the initial one, yet clear victories were attained by the three Federalist standard-bearers, Benjamin West, Samuel Livermore, and Nicholas Gilman. However, when West resigned a third round had to be scheduled; the event was eventually won by

Abiel Foster. Some 3,094 voters (12.9 percent) appeared this time, a far smaller turnout than the first effort, but larger than the second.

RHODE ISLAND

For Rhode Island, voting statistics for the Revolutionary era are much less abundant than for the late provincial period. Nevertheless, results obtained from the gubernatorial elections in several towns permit some estimate to be made of the overall turnout. In general, it would seem that the number participating was much smaller than during the Ward–Hopkins controversy (1755–70), yet was still considerable at times. Although not many of the adult males voted regularly in the war years, 25 to 35 percent took part amid the heated factional struggles of the late 1780s. If we use only qualified electors as the standard, then nearly 60 percent—perhaps a higher proportion than in any other state—were active voters at that point.

From 1777 to 1780, not more than 15 percent of the adult men cast ballots in each year's general election. Records from 17 of the state's 29 towns show 890 votes received in the 1778 contest, as William Greene bested William Bradford by a two-to-one margin. In 1780, some 883 votes can be counted for a slightly different group of 17 towns, Greene winning this time without formal opposition. For the remainder of the decade extant returns are fewer, yet the nearly complete figures from seven towns comprising about one-third of the population—Coventry, Exeter, Johnston, Newport, Providence, Warren, and West Greenwich—make possible a rough projection of the entire turnout on each occasion. Only 13.5 percent of the adult males voted in these seven locales in 1781, but conflict over the impost and other issues helped to stimulate rises in 1782 and 1783 to 22.5 and 24.4 percent, respectively. The next two elections (1784 and 1785), when no really crucial matters were at stake, saw a significant drop, with merely 10.6 and 12.4 percent attending.

However, in 1786, the battle over the issuance of paper currency and the appearance of an alternative slate brought more than 30 percent of the adult males to the polls as paper-money candidate John Collins topped longtime incumbent William Greene. The vote in Coventry increased from 91 to 199, in West Greenwich from 61 to 149, and in Newport from 77 to 210. A year later, in 1787, an even greater number came out: approximately 4,170 statewide, amounting to one-third of the adult men and almost three-fifths of the bona fide freemen. In this race Collins defeated William Bradford, a hard-money advocate, 2,969 to 1,141. Less than half as many persons (16.2 percent in the seven towns) were present for the 1788 gubernatorial contest as in the previous year, though 25.5 percent, a somewhat larger proportion, handed in tickets for the event in 1789.[3]

One other instance of balloting in Rhode Island should be noted. In what amounted to a popular referendum on the federal Constitution in the spring of 1788, some 2,945 men (24.4 percent) participated and rendered a verdict—237 yeas, 2,708 nays. While lower than the previous year's gubernatorial total, this was a fairly sizable figure under the circumstances, for the Federalists had boycotted the election in certain mercantile centers; just eleven votes were recorded in Newport, and but one in Providence. To illustrate the heavy rate of turnout, thirteen of the state's thirty towns could boast that 30 percent or more of its adult males had taken a stand on the document. The new community of Foster (with 45 percent) and Little Compton (with 42.4 percent) produced the two highest tallies (see table 2).[4]

PENNSYLVANIA

Pennsylvania returns, though far from complete, provide a fairly good estimate of the quantity of voters taking part each year. They show that, in spite of low turnouts for the early war period, the rate of participation reached 20 percent of the adult males by the beginning of the 1780s, and 25 to 35 percent at the end of that decade. These were respectable amounts considering that the governor was not elected; only legislators and county officials appeared on the ballot. Growing factional competition between the Republicans and Constitutionalists, an increase in the number of polling places, and eventual repeal of the test laws were probably most responsible for the rise.

Wartime dislocations and the loyalty oath held down the proportion of active voters for quite a while. Only about 10 to 15 percent of the adult men appeared at the ballot box for the statewide elections of 1777, 1778, and 1779. The acceleration of the factional

TABLE 2

Rhode Island Referendum on the Federal Constitution, 1788

Town	Yeas	Nays	Total	Percentage of Adult White Males
Barrington	9	34	43	34.1
Bristol	26	23	49	20.0
Charlestown	6	51	57	21.5
Coventry	0	180	180	37.1
Cranston	0	101	101	28.9
Cumberland	10	113	123	32.8
East Greenwich	2	91	93	27.9
Exeter	6	136	142	31.8
Foster	0	177	177	45.0
Gloucester	9	228	237	32.1
Hopkinton	33	95	128	32.3
Jamestown	5	11	16	21.1
Johnston	1	79	80	32.4
Little Compton	63	57	120	42.4
Middletown	6	40	46	27.5
Newport	1	10	11	1.0
New Shoreham	0	32	32	26.0
North Kingstown	2	160	162	35.0
North Providence	0	48	48	24.4
Portsmouth	12	60	72	23.3
Providence	0	1	1	0.1
Richmond	1	68	69	25.4
Scituate	0	156	156	36.6
Smithfield	2	158	160	26.7
South Kingstown	1	125	126	21.0
Tiverton	23	92	115	26.6
Warren	2	41	43	20.0
Warwick	3	140	143	32.6
Westerly	12	56	68	19.1
West Greenwich	2	145	147	37.1
Totals	237	2,708	2,945	24.4

struggle in 1780, leading to Republican ascendancy, attracted 18 to 20 percent to the polls that year, and similar percentages were achieved in both 1781 and 1782. With the war fully over and new issues emerging, totals climbed even higher in 1783. Some 17,000 electors (24.8 percent of the adult males) handed in tickets that year. The greatest outpouring of votes occurred in Cumberland and York counties and in the city of Philadelphia, districts which would continue to accumulate the biggest amounts on most subsequent occasions. Cumberland, in fact, sometimes surpassed the 60 percent mark.

Although competition became even heavier, the tallies seem to have fallen off a bit in 1784 and 1785. About 16,000 men (22 to 23 percent) polled each time in some of the closest races the state had seen. In 1785, for example, the Republicans defeated the Constitutionalists in the city of Philadelphia by merely one hundred votes, while the latter won in Northumberland by less than twenty. The removal of all test laws resulted in a much larger showing in 1786 as more than 20,300 voters (27.3 percent of the adult males) attended. The Republicans must have captured the bulk of the new element, for they won in certain counties by a two-to-one margin.

In 1787, the assembly figure was somewhat smaller (19,400 or 24.9 percent) since the Republicans were now in command and their opponents put up little resistance. Then, in the special election held later that year, the count diminished even further. The contest for choosing delegates to the state ratifying convention brought out only 13,000 of the 70,000 freemen—18.6 percent (or 16.7 percent of the 78,000 adult males). One of the few available local returns, that for the city of Philadelphia, shows half the usual sum, just 1,350 votes. Others, for Berks, Lancaster, and York, were proportionately no higher. The 1788 legislative elections saw approximately 20,400 men (25 percent of the adult males) casting ballots, yet the first congressional election that winter drew far fewer people (14,655, or 18 percent). A short time afterward, only 6,800 votes (8 percent) were given for presidential Electors. However, in the fall elections of 1789, when representatives to a state constitutional convention were designated along with assemblymen, an estimated 30,000 persons came to the polls—more than 35 percent, the most sizable turnout of the period (see table 3).[5]

MARYLAND

Turnout in Maryland was rather small during the war years, but it picked up considerably afterward, especially in the late 1780s. The triennial elections for county sheriff (coinciding with the choice of assemblymen), the only ones for which we have complete

TABLE 3

Pennsylvania Elections, 1777–1789

Year	Estimated Number of Voters	Percentage of Adult White Males
1777–79	6,000–9,000	10–15
1780–82	11,500–13,000	18–20
1783	17,000	24.8
1784	16,000	22.7
1785	16,000	22.1
1786	20,300	27.3
1787	19,400	24.9
1787[a]	13,000	16.7
1788	20,400	25.0
1788[b]	14,655	18.0
1789[c]	6,800	8.0
1789[d]	30,000	35.3

[a] Election of delegates to state ratifying convention
[b] Election of first federal congressmen
[c] Choice of presidential Electors
[d] Included choice of delegates to state constitutional convention

data, clearly demonstrate this change. While only about 15 percent of the adult white males voted in these contests in 1779, the figure increased to 23.5 percent in 1782, 26.5 percent in 1785, and 32.9 percent in 1788 (see table 4). The paper money issue and rising factionalism helped to bring more and more voters to the polls, ultimately giving the state one of the highest rates of participation.

Various other returns illustrate Maryland's upward surge in the last half of the 1780s. In 1786, over 41 percent of the adult white males turned out for the assembly contest in Anne Arundel County, including thirteen voters who "at the risque of their lives, braved the mighty flood and swam their horses across Patuxent." A year later, in 1787, almost 30 percent took part in Baltimore town, and 43 percent did so in Baltimore county. No exact overall statistics are available for the choice of delegates to the constitutional ratifying convention in the spring of 1788; one report claims that only 6,000 votes were cast statewide—just 15–20 percent of the white men and no more than 25 percent of the eligible voters. Yet the count was very sizable in certain locales: around 43 percent in the town of Baltimore and 48.8 percent in Montgomery County, for example. If the tally was smaller in most other districts (20.9 percent in Baltimore County, 21.5 percent in Harford County, and 23.9 percent in Washington County), it may have been due to the one-sided nature of the contests.

The largest turnout of the period occurred at the regular state elections in the fall of 1788, as factional strife became more severe. Nearly 14,000 votes (approximately 33 percent) were recorded, with 46.4 percent polling in Harford County, 55.6 percent in Kent County, and 57.9 percent in Baltimore County. Three months later, in January, 1789, in the balloting for the first federal Congress, there was a signficant drop in the total, perhaps because of

TABLE 4

Number of Votes in Maryland Sheriff Elections, 1779, 1782, 1785, and 1788

County	1779	1782	1785	1788
Anne Arundel	292	436	633	678
Baltimore	452	1,309	1,616	2,317
Calvert	241	118	322	382
Caroline	83	204	351	419
Cecil	218	431	291	483
Charles	491	361	548	767
Dorchester	274	334	426	728
Frederick	333	409	352	1,560
Harford	425	892	875	1,067
Kent	345	608	712	835
Montgomery	221	472	289	405
Prince George	448	640	1,028	912
Queen Anne's	182	478	540	578
St. Mary's	551	408	518	459
Somerset	106	98	293	268
Talbot	123	146	260	360
Washington	227	467	625	1,020
Worcester	216	206	426	628
Totals	5,228	8,017	10,105	13,866

bad weather or because of the predominance of the Federalists. Only about 8,000 voters (18.3 percent) came out, and just one county, Washington, registered more than twice the statewide average, with 38.9 percent.[6]

MASSACHUSETTS

In Massachusetts, where abundant town-by-town figures have been preserved for most statewide elections after 1780, it seems that few men regularly voted, at least before 1787. The absence of well-defined factions and alternative slates, along with different dates for gubernatorial, assembly, and local contests, were probably the key factors in keeping turnouts low. To be sure, a fairly substantial number—16,235 or 23 percent of the adult males—registered their approval of the state constitution in 1780. But merely 10.6 to 17.3 percent of the adult males participated in the annual choice of governor between 1780 and 1786, and probably even fewer went to the polls for the other races. Beginning in 1787, however, controversial issues and more clear-cut factionalism sparked a precipitous rise in the number of those casting ballots (see table 5).

TABLE 5

**Massachusetts Gubernatorial Elections,
1780–1789**

Year	Number of Voters	Percentage Turnout	Votes Received by Winner		Percentage Received by Winner
1780	12,281	17.3	Hancock	11,207	91.3
1781	8,585	12.1	Hancock	7,996	93.1
1782	7,744	10.8	Hancock	5,855	75.6
1783	9,108	12.7	Hancock	. . .	. . .
1784	7,631	10.6	Hancock	. . .	. . .
1785	9,065	11.9	Bowdoin	3,510	38.7
1786	8,231	10.3	Bowdoin	6,001	72.9
1787	24,588	29.3	Hancock	18,459	75.1
1788	22,157	25.2	Hancock	17,841	80.5
1789	21,384	23.3	Hancock	17,264	80.7

The first five gubernatorial elections (1780–84) were all won easily by John Hancock, who maintained his popularity with the electorate in spite of growing criticism by the Bowdoin–Warren clique. He received 11,207 out of 12,281 votes (91.3 percent) in 1780, 7,996 out of 8,585 (93.1 percent) in 1781, and 5,855 out of 7,744 (75.6 percent) in 1782. While no complete statistics are available for 1783 and 1784, it would appear from the fragmentary returns that Hancock triumphed both times by similarly large margins. In 1785, when Hancock stepped down, the state's first real contest occurred, though it caused only a slight increase in turnout, as 11.9 percent came to the polls compared to 10.6 percent on the prior occasion. Merchant James Bowdoin secured about 39 percent of the 9,065 votes, former lieutenant governor Thomas Cushing 33 percent, and General Benjamin Lincoln 13 percent, with Bowdoin being designated governor by the upper house. The following year (1786), despite growing economic problems, the count fell to 10.3 percent. Bowdoin, having little competition, garnered 72.9 percent of the overall tally (6,001 of 8,231) and carried every county except Bristol and Lincoln.

In 1787, agitation over Shays's Rebellion and other issues plus John Hancock's return to political life brought out almost three times as many voters as in the previous year. Some 24,588 persons (29.3 percent of the adult males) took part, ousting Bowdoin and his followers in the biggest changeover of the decade, with Hancock capturing three-fourths of the total. The few available results for the selection of delegates to the state ratifying convention show approximately 27 percent attended. The large eastern towns of Boston, Charlestown, and Marblehead recorded around 25 percent, though the smaller western towns of Sheffield, Great Barrington, and Worcester produced 43.2, 44.9, and 45.7 percent, respectively.

The gubernatorial vote remained fairly high in 1788 (22,157, or 25.2 percent) as Hancock, with both Federalist and moderate support, overwhelmed Antifederalist candidate Elbridge Gerry, acquiring almost 81 percent to Gerry's 19 percent. In 1789, Hancock, now running with Samuel Adams, defeated James Bowdoin and Benjamin Lincoln, again taking 81 percent. Expectation of easy victory probably contributed to the continuing reduction in turnout—to 23.3 percent. But interest in the governor's race was still larger than that for the first federal elections a few months earlier. Only 8,815 (10 percent) participated in the naming of presidential Electors, and just 11,510 (13.1 percent) were present for the initial balloting in the congressional races. However, in those counties where run-offs were required in the choice of congressmen, considerably higher percentages were sometimes achieved. Approximately 30 percent polled in Worcester, and 26.3 percent did so in the Hampshire-Berkshire district in the third rounds of each contest.[7]

CONNECTICUT

Connecticut returns are not as complete as one might wish, though overall totals are available for most of the gubernatorial elections of the 1780s. These indicate that on the average only about 15 percent of the adult males went to the polls for the eight contests recorded (1780–84 and 1786–88). The lack of widespread factionalism outside the legislature and a political tradition which normally called for the reelection of incumbents help to account for the low (15 percent) annual turnout. Actually, on the basis of eligible voters the figure would be much larger, perhaps 25 percent, since not more than three-fifths of the adult men in the state had taken the freeman's oath to qualify.

Unlike other states, the vote in Connecticut was higher in the earlier part of the 1780s than in the later part. Questions about crucial economic matters and Governor Trumbull's wartime leadership stirred up a great deal of public debate at that point. The biggest turnout of the decade was recorded in 1780 (7,266, or 17.9 percent of the adult males) as Trumbull failed to receive a majority for the first time, obtaining just 3,598 votes to 3,668 for several others. He was, however, kept in office, thanks to a favorable nod by the assembly. The same situation occurred in 1781 when 6,802 (or 16.8 percent) came out, and Trumbull acquired only 2,636, or two-fifths, of the ballots cast. Trumbull did amass a bare majority of the popular vote in 1782 (3,026 of 6,032), but in 1783 he had to depend on the lower house once more, getting just 2,209 out of 7,057 votes, with William Pitkin not far behind at 2,080. After Trumbull's retirement in early 1784, a four-way race ensued among Pitkin (1,689), Samuel Huntington (1,177), Oliver Wolcott (1,053), and former Deputy Governor Matthew Griswold (2,192). Since Griswold placed first and had served loyally for many years, he was given the top office by the assembly. In each of these years participation did not vary too widely; approximately 14.9 percent voted in 1782, 17.0 percent in 1783, and 16.1 percent in 1784.

Griswold won the governorship in 1785 (though no figures for this year have been found), and had the highest total again in 1786, accumulating 2,160 votes to Samuel Huntington's 1,701. But since Griswold did not gain a majority of the 5,823 ballots cast and was considered too old to continue, house members chose Huntington to sit in the governor's chair. Huntington won reelection by a landslide in both 1787 and 1788. Although no statistics are preserved for the gubernatorial races, the results for the upper house show a high of 3,833 votes in the first contest and 3,374 in the second. Since the amount of votes cast for governor was usually about 2,000 more, perhaps 5,833 (12.8 percent) and 5,374 (11.6 percent) would be fairly good estimates of the overall tally in those years (see table 6).

The number of voters taking part in the selection of delegates to the Connecticut constitutional ratifying convention was not usually recorded. Nevertheless, the handful of known results indicates that attendance was generally larger than at regular town election meetings. While Lebanon counted only 122 persons (14.6 percent), Durham found 71 (28.2 percent), Farmington 121 (22.3 percent), Hamden 78 (26.1 percent), and Killingworth 150 (31.9 percent). In addition, Woodstock's meetinghouse was said to be "uncommonly full" for the occasion. There are no available figures for the designation of federal Congressmen in early 1789 though some 399 different individuals were reported to have received votes in the nomination process for that office.[8]

NEW YORK

Turnouts in New York prior to the late 1780s were relatively low. According to Abraham Yates not one in ten people voted, though *New York Journal* editor Thomas Greenleaf put it as high as one in four.[9] Probably the average was somewhere in the middle. The small figure resulted from wartime dislocations, a restricted electorate, and the lack of competition in many contests. In New York City, where there were competing tickets, 383 votes were recorded in the assembly election of 1783, 666 votes in 1785, and 552 votes in 1786. None of these represented more than 25 percent of the eligible voters.

Polling at the initial statewide elections was even less impressive. The early gubernatorial races were won easily by George Clinton,

TABLE 6

**Connecticut Gubernatorial Elections,
1780–1788**

	Number of Votes	Percentage of Adult White Males		Number of Votes	Percentage of Adult White Males
1780			**1784**		
J. Trumbull	3,598[a]		M. Griswold	2,192[a]	
Scattered	3,668		W. Pitkin	1,689	
	7,266	17.9	S. Huntington	1,177	
			O. Wolcott	1,053	
1781			Scattered	742	
J. Trumbull	2,636[a]			6,853	16.1
W. Pitkin	1,225				
Scattered	2,941		**1786**		
	6,802	16.8	M. Griswold	2,160	
			S. Huntington	1,701[a]	
1782			O. Wolcott	1,049	
J. Trumbull	3,026		Scattered	913	
Scattered	3,006			5,823	13.1
	6,032	14.9			
			1787		
1783			S. Huntington	c. 5,833	12.8
J. Trumbull	2,209[a]				
W. Pitkin	2,080		**1788**		
O. Wolcott	918		S. Huntington	c. 5,374	11.6
S. Huntington	896				
Scattered	954				
	7,057	17.0			

[a] Chosen governor by the lower house

who faced only minimal opposition except on the first occasion in 1777. In that year, with 3,792 votes counted (about 15 percent of the adult males in unoccupied territory), Clinton obtained 1,828, followed by Philip Schuyler (1,199), John Morin Scott (368), and John Jay (367). The geographical distribution showed Clinton winning in Ulster, Orange, Dutchess, and Westchester, with Schuyler victorious in his home county, Albany, as well as in frontier Tryon and Charlotte, a pattern that would more or less continue throughout the period.

In the next election for governor (1780), perhaps 10 percent took part. Clinton, running virtually unopposed, acquired 3,624 votes, just a few less than the total for all candidates in 1777. Three years later, in 1783, around 5,000 ballots were cast, roughly 15 percent of the adult white males, with Clinton getting 3,584, Schuyler only 643 (mostly in Albany County), and Ephraim Paine 520 (mostly in Dutchess County). Although no figures are known for 1786, when Clinton again won handily, it is probable that the vote remained at the same low level. Yet, in 1789, when the Federalists challenged Clinton and campaigned strongly for his opponent, Robert Yates, some 12,353 electors came out (18.5 percent of the adult men, or 34.2 percent of the eligible voters), with Clinton barely defeating Yates, 6,391 to 5,962. Approximately the same number of votes (about 12,000) were recorded shortly afterward in the first congressional contest as each side captured three seats.

Actually, the state's biggest turnout occurred a year earlier in the election of delegates to the constitutional ratifying convention. Full manhood suffrage was permitted and more than 24,500 persons went to the polls, nearly 43.4 percent. New York City registered 48.4 percent, Albany 52.0 percent, and Columbia County 63.5 percent. They were followed by Montgomery County 42.4 percent, Dutchess County 35.4 percent, Queens County 34.7 percent, Ulster County 27.9 percent, Westchester County 25.2 percent, and Orange County 10.6 percent. High totals were also achieved in the accompanying assembly election even though property qualifications were invoked. Some 31.8 percent voted in the five counties where data are available—Albany, Columbia, New York, Orange, and Queens.[10]

NEW JERSEY

The handful of returns for New Jersey indicates a very wide disparity in turnout. As few as 7.5 percent and as many as 66.6 percent participated in the legislative elections for which results have been uncovered (see table 7). The size of the vote was influenced by the degree of factionalism present. In addition, higher totals generally occurred where several polling places were available, lower ones

TABLE 7

**New Jersey Legislative Elections, 1782–1788,
and Congressional Election, 1789**

Year	County	Number of Voters	Percentage of Adult White Males
1782	Hunterdon	1,239	33.7
1783	Burlington	347	11.0
1784	Hunterdon	1,072	29.2
1785	Essex	1,790	66.6
	Hunterdon	1,583	43.1
	Monmouth	532	18.1
	Sussex	734	25.9
1787	Burlington	258	7.5
1788	Essex	1,225	35.3
1789	Bergen	366	16.0
	Burlington	2,826	76.4
	Essex	2,984	86.0
	Hunterdon	1,351	34.0
	Middlesex	915	28.6
	Monmouth	606	19.7
	Morris	1,392	42.5
	Somerset	992	44.0
	Gloucester	2,500	95.1
	Salem	886	41.3

where few were available. Essex County, with three locations, reached a 35 percent level in 1788 and a 66.6 percent turnout in 1785. Hunterdon, also with multiple polls, showed an average of 1,300 voters (35.3 percent) for three contests. On the other hand, Burlington, having but one balloting spot, saw only 11 percent and 7.5 percent present for the elections of 1783 and 1787, respectively.

No figures are available for the choice of delegates to the state ratifying convention (1787), though the tally was undoubtedly low because of minimal competition. But in the first congressional race in early 1789, a major increase in the number of polling sites and in the amount of time the polls were open, plus widespread campaigning by the West Jersey Junto and its opponents, led to an enormous expansion of the vote. Over 16,000 adult white males (44 percent) came to the polls, with more than 76 percent casting ballots in Burlington and over 86 percent doing so in Essex and Gloucester. James Schureman topped the victorious Junto ticket with 12,537 votes; Lambert Cadwalader had 8,685, Elias Boudinot 8,603, and Thomas Sinnickson 8,240.[11]

DELAWARE

In Delaware, very few voting totals have come to light for the Revolutionary period and those available are difficult to evaluate. Some of them indicate a rather sizable turnout in this politically divided state; others are less supportive of that conclusion. The legislative election in October, 1776, shows that approximately 19.4 percent of the adult males participated statewide (27.1 percent in Kent, 20.6 percent in Sussex, and 10.9 percent in New Castle). Perhaps the fear of violence kept more people from going to the polls on that occasion, and, along with the "test" oath, continued to hold down numbers for the duration of the war. In subsequent years, as the factional struggle resumed, the tally undoubtedly rose. For example, almost 1,300 (more than 47 percent) cast ballots in New Castle in 1785. Some 655 names were recorded in the controversial Sussex poll in 1787 for delegates to the state ratifying convention, probably two-thirds of those present. Yet when conflict temporarily abated after the federal Constitution was approved, the output fell precipitously. Only 163 men (5.1 percent) attended New Castle's first congressional election in January, 1789, and not many more (320 or 11 percent) appeared at the same contest in Kent County. However, the choice of state officers later that year brought out 1,022 voters (34.5 percent) in Kent and 1,035 (31.5 percent) in Sussex, and figures would increase further in the early 1790s.[12]

VIRGINIA

Although statistical data are rather limited, turnout in Virginia seems to have declined during the Revolutionary era, at least in the first decade after independence. George Mason claimed that "elections are now so little attended to, that a factious, bawling Fellow, who will make a noise four or five miles around him, and prevail upon his party to attend, may carry an Election against a Man of ten times his weight and Influence in the County."[13] In Essex County, the only one for which a considerable number of returns are available, assembly contests before 1776 averaged 343 votes, whereas those for the years 1777 to 1786 averaged 224, with but 112 men voting in 1778. The few other known figures indicate a similar lack of interest. In 1786, merely 149 voters took part in Fairfax (8.7 percent of the adult white males) and only 183 did so in Stafford (17.1 percent).

The reasons for the drop in Virginia voting are hard to pinpoint. Perhaps the introduction of annual elections played a role, as did the lack of factionalism in many areas. However, the paper money issue and the crisis over the Constitution seem to have caused a sizable increase in some counties beginning to 1787. In that year, 387 electors (53.5 percent) went to the polls in Essex, one and one-half times as many as on the previous occasion. Some 663 men (36.1 percent) voted in Accomac, and 282 (30.2 percent) in Princess Anne. The following year (1788), 351 (48.3 percent) participated in Essex and 337 (33.1 percent) were present in Buckingham for the assembly elections. Fairly high totals were also achieved in the regular legislative contests in 1789—43.4 percent in Essex, 36.3 percent in Orange, and 24.7 percent in Princess Anne.

The special elections at the end of the decade—despite their national importance—did not bring about any further rise in voter participation. In fact, the results were slightly lower than for the known assembly competition. The choice of members to the state ratifying convention in the spring of 1788 produced an average turnout of 26.5 percent for the seven counties recorded. The designation of presidential Electors in a dozen counties in early 1789 shows that 16.1 percent of the voters went to the polls. A short while later the first congressional race brought out 21.1 percent in the eight-county Norfolk District and 22.6 percent in twelve other counties, eight of which were in the district fought over by James Madison and James Monroe. Ironically, in Culpeper County, the one where the two men spent most of their time campaigning, just 13.3 percent cast ballots, the lowest proportion anywhere in the area (see table 8).[14]

TABLE 8

Virginia Elections, 1786–1789

Year	County	Number of Voters	Percentage of Adult White Males
1786	Stafford	183	17.1
	Essex	255	35.1
	Fairfax	149	8.7
	Orange	259	26.4
1787	Accomac	663	36.1
	Essex	387	53.3
	Princess Anne	282	30.2
1788	Buckingham	337	33.1
	Essex	351	48.3
1788[a]	Amherst	334	20.3
	Buckingham	337	33.1
	Essex	217	29.9
	Frederick	191	6.2
	Henrico	379	26.0
	Orange	235	22.3
	Princess Anne	270	28.9
1789[b]	Albemarle	180	13.2
	Amherst	270	16.4
	Buckingham	161	15.8
	Culpeper	203	7.5
	Essex	217	29.9
	Fairfax	234	13.7
	Fluvanna	81	17.2
	Isle of Wight	281	29.1
	Northampton	119	17.3
	Orange	117	11.1
	Spotsylvania	278	25.6
	Westmoreland	119	18.3
1789[c]	Albemarle	279	20.5
	Amherst	391	23.8
	Culpeper	359	13.3
	Cumberland	181	25.6
	Essex	108	14.9
	Fluvanna	105	22.3
	Goochland	265	32.2
	Greensville	60	11.2
	Louisa	342	44.6

TABLE 8—*Continued*

Year	County	Number of Voters	Percentage of Adult White Males
	Orange	225	21.3
	Princess Anne	272	29.1
	Spotsylvania	304	27.9
1789	Essex	315	43.4
	Orange	383	36.3
	Princess Anne	231	24.7

[a] Election of delegates to state ratifying convention
[b] Choice of presidential Electors
[c] Choice of first federal congressmen

NORTH CAROLINA

Just a few scattered results have been uncovered from North Carolina, almost all of them for towns, and almost all showing substantial numbers voting. Wilmington counted 83 persons at the polls in 1780, about a 74 percent turnout of the adult white males, though only 35 men (31.3 percent) appeared there in 1783. Hillsborough had 25 voters in 1782, Edenton 66 voters in 1785 (over 45 percent), and New Bern 149 voters in 1787. Orange County produced a total of 650 in the year 1784, approximately 33 percent. The only other known tally comes from the disputed election of delegates to the state ratifying convention in 1788 in Dobbs County. On that occasion, some 372 persons (40 percent) had given in their tickets before dissident Federalists ran off with the ballot box.[15]

SOUTH CAROLINA

Few South Carolina returns are available for the Revolutionary era but, as in earlier times, turnout seems low. One return for St. Andrew's Parish (1783) shows only eleven voters participating, and other returns were probably just as small. The main exception was the city of Charleston, which accumulated several sizable totals. Some 241 voters took part in the municipal election of 1783, 514 in 1784, and 275 in 1787. Assembly contests in 1786 and 1788 drew 426 and 510 votes, respectively (22.4 and 26.8 percent of the adult white males). Approximately 424 tickets (22.3 percent) were handed in for the designation of members to the state ratifying convention in the spring of 1788, and 664 (34.9 percent) were counted in the selection of the first federal representatives later that year (see table 9).

The first congressional race affords us the only overall picture of the vote in this state. Although no exact figures are known (just the tally for each winning candidate), the absence of competition in most districts makes it permissible to equate the victor's tally with the full total. About 3,500 ballots were cast in all, representing 12.2 percent of the adult white males. The biggest turnout occurred in the Charleston District, where some 1,280 persons (31.6 percent) came to the polls. William Loughton Smith amassed 653 votes in defeating Alexander Gillon and Dr. David Ramsay. The Georgetown and Cheraw District had the second largest proportion—15 percent—with Daniel Huger receiving 496. Other districts' amounts included Beaufort and Orangeburgh, 11.8 percent (Aedanus Burke highest with 422); Camden, 9.1 percent (Thomas Sumter highest with 507); and Ninety-Six, 6.3 percent (Thomas T. Tucker highest with 759).[16]

TABLE 9

Charleston, South Carolina, Elections, 1783–1788

Type	Year	Number of Voters	Percentage of Adult White Males
Municipal	1783	241	12.7
	1784	514	27.1
	1787	275	14.5
Assembly	1786	426	22.4
	1788	510	26.8
State Ratifying Convention	1788	424	22.3
Congressional	1788	664	34.9

GEORGIA

Returns from Georgia during the Confederation are few, yet it would appear that turnouts were generally small. A report from the Camden District in 1784 noted that just nine electors had come to the polls: "Mr. [Lachlan] McIntosh had Eight votes and Mr. Davies one and that is said to be by himself."[17] Probably the only area that regularly produced an appreciable total was Chatham County, containing the city of Savannah. Approximately 270 (39.9 percent of the adult white males) participated at the assembly contest in Chatham in 1783, and 246 (36.3 percent) did so in 1784. The highest amount was recorded there in 1787 when 401 persons (59.2 percent) attended the election, which included the choice of delegates to the state ratifying convention. The second highest came in 1788 as 337 (49.8 percent) voted not only for assemblymen but for representatives to a state constitutional convention as well.[18] The one other known result is the 270 voters (18.7 percent) for ratifying convention members in Burke County in 1787.

A NOTE ON TURNOUT FOR THE FIRST NATIONWIDE ELECTIONS

It is difficult to make a judgment about the proportion of voters in the special elections of the late 1780s—the naming of delegates to the constitutional ratifying conventions (1787-88) and the choice of congressmen and presidential Electors (1788-89). Complete figures for each race exist in only a few cases, some states having no data at all. In the ratification vote, very fragmentary returns from Massachusetts and Virginia show approximately 27 percent of the adult white males taking part. The Rhode Island referendum drew 24.4 percent. Contemporary estimates in Pennsylvania and Maryland work out to 16.7 percent and 15 percent, respectively. Only in New York, where property qualifications were not invoked, did the total surpass 40 percent. The historian Forrest McDonald was probably being generous when he asserted that about one man in four voted on the Constitution. Statistics for the first federal elections are slightly more abundant, though overall turnout was possibly smaller. New Jersey achieved an amazing 44 percent in the congressional contest, but next on the list is New Hampshire, with 21.4 percent. These states are followed by New York (18.5 percent), Maryland (18.3 percent), Pennsylvania (18 percent), Massachusetts (13.1

percent), and South Carolina (12.2 percent). The results for presidential Electors must have been even lower if the statistics of 16.8 percent in New Hampshire, 10 percent in Massachusetts, and 8 percent in Pennsylvania are any indication.[19]

Although the vote on these momentous occasions was less than one might expect, and in certain cases smaller than that for the annual state contests, the returns do not necessarily indicate widespread apathy. In a number of places the figures rose higher than ever before and would have been higher still had not suffrage requirements been so restrictive. Also, turnout was limited by the fact that these were not regularly scheduled elections and often occurred in the midst of winter, a very inopportune time. Most significant, however, was the lack of real competition in many areas. Even when a state was politically divided, the people within a particular voting district frequently aligned themselves on one side or the other. The records show that a majority of towns and counties were either solidly Federalist or almost all Antifederalist. Candidates in this situation ordinarily ran unopposed, so that even normally active electors had little reason to go to the polls. As a correspondent in Washington County, Maryland (where the vote for convention delegates was rather low), pointed out: "Had any thing like a respectable Opposition taken place in the Election, 1500 Federal Votes would have been taken on this Occasion, as the Inhabitants, even in the remotest Parts of the County, held themselves in Readiness, had their Assistance been requisite."[20]

8

Voting Behavior

★★★★★★★★★★★★★★

Voting behavior in the Revolutionary era is not an easy subject to analyze. Why did people vote? What accounted for the size of a particular turnout or the selection of one individual over another? Just as was true for the provincial period, data here are extremely fragmentary. In fact, fewer poll lists and related sources of information are available for the 1780s than for the 1760s.[1] Nevertheless, existing evidence allows certain tentative conclusions to be drawn concerning two chief aspects: the extent of the vote and the reasons for partisan choice. Several systematic and ecological variables—suffrage qualifications, geographic and economic influences, etc.—can be measured to some degree. Other elements, such as the importance of candidates and issues, though not so readily subject to examination, still provide clues to why voters at that time acted in the manner they did.

Before making any assessment of variables, however, a few general points should be noted. To begin with, voting in the dozen years after independence was not seen as the significant political act it has since become. While growing numbers were taking part in the process, the majority of electors still did not regularly cast ballots. Some of them probably felt either too preoccupied or too isolated to do so. Others may have had difficulty perceiving the ways in which a vote could affect their lives. They may have found little to choose between candidates and the idea of influencing policy through the ballot box may have appeared remote to them. Of course, among persons who did exercise their franchise rights, many believed that clear choices did exist and that their votes did carry weight. Admittedly, for certain people election day had more social than political meaning. After all, going to the polls provided a break from seemingly unending work, a time to get together with old friends. Yet contemporary reports coupled with large fluctuations in the returns would seem to indicate that most individuals who attended elections did so for other than social reasons.

In regard to turnout in the different states, numerous factors affected its size on any given occasion. Among systematic variables perhaps the most important of these were the suffrage requirements. Suffrage laws, although liberalized in many states, still sharply restricted the proportion of voters. Not only were most blacks and women barred, but a sizable number of white men also continued to be excluded by certain provisions. The freeman's oath in Rhode Island and Connecticut probably cut totals there by as much as one-third. Property qualifications, while lower than before, reduced participation by at least 5 to 10 percent and perhaps more. One can gauge what the vote might have been without property limits by looking at the New York election of 1788, in which all adult white males were permitted to choose delegates to the constitutional ratifying convention. The tally in several counties was considerably larger for this contest than for the concurrent designation of assemblymen, where property standards were in effect. In Albany, about 7,400 men cast ballots for convention members, yet only 4,900 took part in the assembly poll. New York City's convention figure of approximately 2,850 was nearly twice that (1,650) recorded for the assembly race. The difference in some areas, however, was comparatively small; Orange County, for example, had 340 convention voters and 300 assembly voters.[2]

The type of officeholders to be selected also had some influence upon the quantity of votes. The fact that governors were popularly chosen in many of the northern states partly explains why turnout was higher in that region than in the South. The choice of several kinds of officials on the same day invariably lifted the totals in the locales which followed that course. The election of county sheriffs, coroners, and assessors in conjunction with assemblymen in Pennsylvania and Delaware helps to account to some degree for heavy participation in those two places. In New Hampshire, the designation of the chief executive at the annual town meeting in March, when senators and local officers were also being named, certainly contributed to its amassing the highest percentage gubernatorial vote of any state in the Confederation era.[3]

Most states held separate local and statewide elections and it is difficult to compare turnouts for each kind since statistics for the former are very scarce. Massachusetts, having chosen town officers in March, governor, lieutenant governor, and senators in April, and representatives in May, provides some basis for comparison. In the city of Boston, where a number of figures have been uncovered, the vote for governor was usually higher than the vote for assemblymen, which in turn was higher than the vote for local officials. On only one occasion, in 1786, did the latter total surpass both of the others. In Worcester, however, several more instances of larger local tallies can be found. From 1784 to 1786, town meeting returns were greater than the gubernatorial poll in all three cases. But in 1787, when the Commonwealth became plagued by political turmoil and crucial statewide issues seemed at stake, the situation was reversed, and almost twice as many came out for the governor's race (see table 10).[4]

The proximity of the ballot box was another important determinant upon the size of the vote. Turnout in some southern states was undoubtedly limited by the fact that voting still occurred only at the county seat, a long distance away for many people. In the Middle States, on the other hand, the gradual increase in the number of polling places after 1776 surely added to the count in certain areas. New Jersey's Burlington County, which continued to have just one voting spot, averaged little more than 10 percent turnout, whereas Hunterdon and Essex, each containing several polling places, produced amounts ranging from 35 to 67 percent for assembly contests. Although no statistical evaluation can be made for New York and Pennsylvania, it is probable that the higher totals recorded there in the late 1780s were partly the result of newly created voting sites and better access to the polls.[5]

As in earlier years, the urban voter, closer to the ballot box and better informed, was more likely to participate at election time than the rural voter. The turnout in cities such as Baltimore, Boston, New York, and Philadelphia generally ranked among the highest in their respective states. If only qualified electors are considered, Newport and Providence surpassed all the smaller agrarian communities in Rhode Island. While data are somewhat lacking, it would appear that the overall count in Charleston, South Carolina, Savannah, Georgia, and the towns of North Carolina was comparatively greater as well. Indeed, it is probable that the gap between

TABLE 10

Local and Statewide Returns, Boston and
Worcester, Massachusetts, 1780–1789

Year	Governor's Total	Assemblymen's Total	Local Total
BOSTON			
1780	923	185	. . .
1781	513	438	. . .
1782	607	350	. . .
1783	859	378	153
1784	571	402	280
1785	951	502	. . .
1786	780	762	836
1787	1,499	630	379
1788	1,432	815	281
1789	1,835	658	286
WORCESTER			
1780	77	. . .	. . .
1781	53	. . .	. . .
1782	49	90	. . .
1783	. . .	. . .	. . .
1784	44	. . .	113
1785	72	. . .	77
1786	49	. . .	104
1787	178	. . .	94
1788	130	. . .	116
1789	. . .	. . .	. . .

the urban and rural vote was wider in the southern states than in the northern ones. In the single statewide tally available for South Carolina—the congressional election of 1788—the percentage for Charleston stood two to three times above that of any other district.[6]

Turnouts were larger not only in the urban centers, but in the surrounding areas as well. That is, the older, well-established coastal counties close to the major cities usually outdrew the more newly-settled frontier regions, and by a substantial amount. Although we have few related statistics for the South, those existing for the northern states definitely bear this out. In Massachusetts, Suffolk and Middlesex counties (in the vicinity of Boston) regularly achieved a much higher percentage than counties a great distance from the capital. The two nearby counties, containing about 18 percent of the population, contributed roughly 30 percent of the state vote; three equivalent outlying counties—Berkshire, Cumberland, and Lincoln—supplied but 10 to 15 percent. New Hampshire's more developed eastern counties—Rockingham, Hillsborough, and Strafford—provided that state's heaviest balloting, whereas Grafton and Cheshire, both located in the interior, furnished the lightest (see table 11). To be sure, some exceptions occurred at times. Upstate New York's Columbia and Montgomery counties reached very sizable figures in the election of delegates to the ratifying convention in 1788, but such results were unusual.[7]

Another important influence upon the volume of popular response was the degree of political maturity and factionalism present. Factions, by bringing political matters to public attention and

TABLE 11

Percentage Turnout for Selected Massachusetts and New Hampshire Counties, 1785–1789

County	Percentage of State's Adult White Males Residing in County	1785	1786	1787	1788	1789
MASSACHUSETTS						
Berkshire	6.1	7.7	7.4	4.3	6.3	4.2
Cumberland (Me.)	5.2	2.3	1.9	2.2	3.3	4.4
Lincoln (Me.)	6.5	1.0	2.4	2.0	4.2	6.7
Middlesex	9.2	15.5	14.4	15.5	12.9	12.6
Suffolk	9.5	15.2	17.7	15.7	13.2	15.8
NEW HAMPSHIRE						
Cheshire	19.4	15.0	14.3	17.9	14.7	18.1
Grafton	10.4	5.8	6.8	5.0	6.2	6.7
Hillsborough	22.6	23.5	20.8	26.8	27.0	18.9
Rockingham	30.9	39.1	32.5	31.8	35.9	38.4
Strafford	16.7	16.6	25.5	18.5	16.2	17.9

appealing constantly for support, invariably raised the level of balloting. States such as Pennsylvania, with two well-organized, competing groups, generally had much higher tallies than did those states in which factions were less developed and did not extend much beyond the legislature. As factionalism grew in the late 1780s in New York and Rhode Island, a corresponding rise took place in the proportion of voters at the polls. New York's gubernatorial total in 1789 was twice as large as any previous one. Rhode Island's output in 1786 and 1787 was probably three times the amount registered in 1784 and 1785.[8]

In conjunction with factions, significant issues helped draw greater numbers. Many new people came to the ballot box when a contest revolved around a matter closely affecting them. Shays's Rebellion and continued agitation over paper currency led to a tripling of the percentage of participants in Massachusetts in 1787 compared to the previous year. (It is interesting that the increase was larger in the eastern counties such as Essex and Suffolk than in the western counties of Hampshire and Berkshire, the focal point of the protest.) The struggle over paper money also caused bigger turnouts in Maryland. The tallies in Anne Arundel County, for example, climbed from 630 in 1785 to 900 in 1786, as the pro- and anti-paper forces began battling each other. Although statistical evidence is lacking it would appear that the paper-money issue raised totals in Virginia around this time too.[9]

Factionalism and vital issues had the effect of increasing turnout not only for a single election, but over the course of several subsequent ones as well. Once attached to a cause, the voter was more apt to take part on a regular basis. One can best observe this phenomenon in Rhode Island, where a much higher rate of voter continuity evolved in the strife-torn years after 1786 than earlier in the decade when divisions were less pronounced. In the town of Johnston, just outside of Providence, only 16 of the 31 voters (51.6 percent) in 1783 participated again in 1784, whereas 81 of the 107 voters (75.7 percent) in 1786 took part on the next occasion in 1787. Barely one-third (26 of 76, or 34.2 percent) of the active balloters residing there in the years 1781 to 1784 went to the polls three or more times, yet 74 of 132 (56.1 percent) did so from 1786 to 1789.[10]

Though they cannot be measured well quantitatively, certain personal factors—one's attitude toward government, one's ethnic or religious affiliation, and his economic standing—also influenced the amount of voter participation. While some men had a deep sense of public responsibility and exercised their election privileges often, others were not so heavily motivated, and cast ballots far less frequently. Several contemporaries complained of voter apathy and of the people's "fatal omission of their duty." Even those individuals who did go to the polls, they argued, were not always aware of the candidates and the issues. "Few of them enquire any farther than who was in last, and vote for him again; without taking the trouble of examining the consequences," claimed one writer in Massachusetts.[11] In regard to ethnic background, it would seem that those of foreign extraction, especially the Germans and the Dutch, were still less inclined to vote than those of British ancestry. Northampton, Berks, and Lancaster counties in Pennsylvania, containing large concentrations of German-speaking people, rarely experienced a heavy turnout, nor did Ulster and Kings counties in New York, which had considerable numbers of Dutchmen.[12]

A person's economic status probably had a major bearing on his inclination to vote, though positions seem to have been reversed from earlier times. One of the most striking aspects of polling in the provincial period was the higher turnout among the less affluent than among other groups. But evidence from the Confederation years indicates that, as in our own times, the rich were more likely to vote than were the poor or the middle class. In New York City, where an inhabitant needed to possess a one hundred-pound estate to qualify for electing state senators, larger numbers of wealthy voters appeared at the polls than did men with little property, who could choose only assemblymen. While the difference was slight in some cases—24 percent compared to 23 percent in 1785, 21 percent compared to 19 percent in 1786—the figures for 1788 reveal that 69 percent of those above the one hundred-pound level took part, while no more than 48 percent of those below that level participated.[13]

A study by Norman K. Risjord of several Virginia poll lists from the late 1780s demonstrates an even clearer relationship between wealth and the degree of participation. In almost every case, the higher an individual was stationed on the economic ladder, the greater was the likelihood that he would cast a vote. The famous election involving James Madison and James Monroe in Amherst County shows that only 19.1 percent of the least affluent in terms of property (0 to £24) took part, whereas 43.8 percent of the middling group (£75 to £149) voted, as did 60.9 percent of the wealthiest class (over £400). In two 1789 elections in Greensville County,

9.7 percent of the poorest men voted, in comparison to 22.8 percent from the middle ranks, and 43.2 percent of the wealthy. An Accomac County contest held in 1787 had 31.5 percent, 41.4 percent, and 48.2 percent for the three levels, respectively.[14]

In spite of the wealthy's greater propensity to vote than the poor, this did not mean that they formed the primary element at the polls. As Risjord points out, those in attendance usually represented a "fair cross-section" of the county taxpayers. "Indeed, the poorest voters were a majority of the electorate on every occasion," he concludes.[15] Moreoever, there is little evidence that the gentry objected to this situation. Although the law allowed rich planters to vote in each county where they possessed land, few of them ever exercised this privilege. Nor did they engage in any other efforts to curtail the common man's use of the suffrage. Instead, the candidates and their friends devoted all their energy to winning the average freeholder's support.

The chief determinants of partisan choice are as speculative and difficult to quantify as those affecting turnout. In the provincial period, several factors had a major bearing upon which side a man supported. These included factional development, sectional influence, crucial issues, the image of the candidates, and the voter's background, especially his ethnic and religious affiliations. Unfortunately, given the limited data, no overall theory of behavior could be constructed for these years.[16] For the Revolutionary era, for which even less data are available, it is similarly impossible to formulate a general explanation of why individuals voted the way they did. One can, however, examine the various elements noted above and attempt to evaluate the relative importance of each one.

Factional influence upon voter preference was certainly stronger in the years after independence than in earlier times. As factions became more organized and far-reaching, they inevitably exerted a greater impact upon the voter and his choice of candidates. While this cannot be statistically proven, we find, for example, many more instances of straight-ticket voting than in the past. In Pennsylvania, the records from the onset show numerous cases where each party's standard-bearers (Republicans and Constitutionalists) received fairly uniform totals in the balloting. By 1786 and 1787, Rhode Island returns indicate heavy partisanship as well. In 1788 and 1789, Maryland and New York, which had become sharply divided into Federalists and Antifederalists, also achieved fully partisan results in many counties. To be sure, in states such as

Virginia, where factions were not as well developed, one discovers a less orderly pattern. In fact, during the election of members to the state ratifying convention in 1788, at least half a dozen counties chose delegations comprised of one Federalist and one Antifederalist. But in the nation as a whole, the trend was definitely toward individuals taking a particular side.[17]

Along with factional influence, and often closely related to it, geographic or sectional factors were extremely important determinants in some states. Election returns for much of New England illustrate a sharp division between inland agrarian preferences and coastal commercial ones. In Massachusetts gubernatorial contests, James Bowdoin, who had strong mercantile attachments, always got many more votes in eastern trading towns than in less commercially-oriented western towns. In 1785, for example, when Bowdoin secured 39 percent of the entire tally, it included 55 percent in the commercial communities, but just 21 percent in small, agrarian locales. Even in the years Bowdoin was trounced by John Hancock, he still acquired a considerable proportion of the eastern commercial-town vote. He received 33 percent of that vote in 1787 compared to 22 percent overall, and 28 percent of it in 1789 as opposed to 16 percent overall.

The Rhode Island governor's contests in 1786 and 1787, during the paper-money controversy, reveal even more well-defined sectional differences. In 1786, Localist John Collins, who easily defeated longtime incumbent William Greene, obtained over 90 percent of the total in rural towns such as Coventry and Exeter, yet managed less than 47 percent in the main coastal center, Newport. The following year, when Collins beat hard-money candidate William Bradford by a two-to-one margin, he again reached 90 percent in several interior towns, but only 26.9 percent and 15.4 percent, respectively, in the seafaring communities of Newport and Providence. The statewide referendum on the Constitution in 1788, boycotted by the aforementioned commercial towns, further underlines the divisions that existed.

Balloting in the New Hampshire gubernatorial races in the late 1780s seems to have followed geographic lines more closely than in any other state. Outside of a few sparsely settled parts of Cheshire and Grafton counties, voters conformed to a clear-cut regional pattern. Inhabitants of the heavily populated and highly commercial Piscataqua area usually backed General John Sullivan of Dover by a huge majority. The only exception was in the city of Portsmouth,

home of Sullivan's chief adversary, John Langdon. Langdon drew
his main strength away from the coast, especially in communities
along the Merrimac River such as Bedford, Boscawen, Concord,
Dunstable, Manchester, and Plymouth (see table 12). Although
Langdon garnered less than 15 percent of the vote in Strafford
County in the east, he averaged 80 to 90 percent further west in
Hillsborough County.[18]

Just as partisan choice was often based on sectional factors, it
was also linked to conflicting views on issues as well. In fact, the

TABLE 12

New Hampshire Gubernatorial Contests, 1786–1788—
John Sullivan versus John Langdon

PISCATAQUA AREA TOWNS			
	1786	1787	1788
Dover	S 228	S 243	S 178
	L 0	L 1	L 14
Durham	S 222	S 196	S 198
	L 0	L 1	L 28
Newington	S 62	S 53	S 45
	L 7	L 8	L 19
Newmarket	S 120	S 98	S 83
	L 12	L 7	L 33
Portsmouth	S 25	S 120	S 6
	L 135	L 127	L 346
Stratham	S 105	S 66	S 49
	L 2	L 11	L 23
MERRIMAC RIVER TOWNS			
	1786	1787	1788
Bedford	S 0	S 0	S 0
	L 47	L 107	L 68
Boscawen	S 0	S 0	S 0
	L 92	L 112	L 116
Concord	S 1	S 6	S 3
	L 137	L 112	L 107
Dunstable	S 0	S 8	S 25
	L 47	L 28	L 2
Manchester	S 0	S 0	S 0
	L 25	L 12	L 34
Plymouth	S 0	S 0	S 0
	L 63	L 75	L 61

issues themselves may have taken precedence in the minds of the majority of voters. Although it is impossible for us to determine whether most men in these years cast their ballots primarily on the basis of issues, several contemporaries thought they did. The Pennsylvania legislative contest in 1786, wrote one newspaper correspondent, was decided chiefly on the questions of paper money and the revival of the Bank of North America. "On those two points," he said, "the late general election *turned* in every county. In Bucks County, it is confidently asserted that the friends to the prevailing ticket, openly declared they voted only for men who would *restore* the honor and credit of the state, by reviving the Bank."[19] In the state of Virginia, a number of persons saw a candidate's stand on the issue of paper currency as having a decisive influence upon the electors in 1787. For example, it was reported that Parke Goodall won in Hanover County only "after a positive and unalterable declaration in public of his affection for paper money."[20] However, it was not paper money but another matter that supposedly caused John Page to lose to James Monroe in Spotsylvania County. According to John Dawson, "Mr. Page's conduct during the last assembly and his opposition to the tobacco bill lost him his election."[21]

As factions and issues became more powerful determinants the importance of the candidate's background diminished. Increasingly touched by the events around them, people seemed less likely to choose someone simply because he was the leading gentleman in the vicinity. "Men of sense and property have lost much of their influence," declared one writer.[22] In Pennsylvania, according to another source, prominent persons, "however well they acquitted themselves in former trusts," have been "carefully avoided."[23] By the late 1780s, the wealthy Theodore Sedgwick of Stockbridge, Massachusetts, who had been left out of the legislature, saw a war being levied upon "virtue, property, and distinctions in the community."[24] Edmund Randolph of Virginia reported that during the election of 1787 Colonel John Nicholas was "assaulted in Albemarle for the tenor of past politics." At the same time, he added, former governor Benjamin Harrison won his House seat by a mere twenty-two votes after having "disclaimed paper money in the streets of Richmond."[25]

Yet the candidate and the manner in which he conducted himself still exerted a significant influence on many voters, especially when he actively sought to make use of his gentlemanly characteristics.

Easily the best example of this was the wealthy John Hancock, who dominated the Massachusetts governorship during a large part of this era. Hancock was perhaps the first major figure in American politics to consciously cultivate his image among the populace, trying to appear as a friend of the people and as a devoted patriot standing above the factional struggles of the times. He had a "peculiar talent of pleasing the multitude," noted John Quincy Adams.[26] "He visits the coffee-houses of Boston, where are congregated the poorest of the inhabitants—men who get their living by bringing wood and vegetables to the city," stated another observer.[27] Hancock's overwhelming appeal, despite his alleged dodging of issues and lack of executive accomplishments, angered his numerous critics immensely. The most outspoken of these was Mercy Otis Warren, wife of one of Hancock's opponents, who, upon his reelection in 1783 wrote the following: "We have seen a man without abilities idolized by the multitude, and fame on the wing to crown the head of imbecility; we have seen people trifling with the privilege of *election,* and throwing away the glorious opportunity of establishing liberty and independence on the everlasting basis of virtue, we have heard them trumpet the praises of their idol of straw, and sing of sacrifices he never had the courage to make."[28]

As candidates began making a bigger effort to ingratiate themselves among the populace, they were less likely to use overt pressure than in earlier times. Nevertheless, some evidence of continued voter coercion does exist. Particularly during the war years, numerous reports tell of soldiers or civilians interfering with the conduct of elections, compelling Tory sympathizers to flee or to favor Whig standard-bearers. Even after peace was established some persons living in places where oral voting was the norm complained about wealthy landowners using their power over those they held in dependence. A petition from inhabitants of Cumberland County, New Jersey, stated that "men of large estates or who have many debtors may, and we presume often do, influence a great many Voters in an Undue manner."[29] Abraham Yates argued that many of New York's landlord-dominated rural counties were no better than England's rotten boroughs. "What material difference is there," Yates asked, "whether one elector by his own voice sends a Member to parliament, or a manour settled with a hundred or a thousand Tenants, under the influence of one Person (and moved by his insinuation, nod or at least a letter . . . the Tenant [gives] his

vote against his inclination, against his most intimate friend or rela-
tion, to a person the landlord was pleased to nominate)."[30] Of
course, people in most states did not have to face such trying conditions. Even in New York and New Jersey the number of people living under an all-powerful landowner was probably small. Tenantry
existed only in a few areas, and the tenant vote for the landlord was
by no means guaranteed.

Generally, the relationship of one's status and wealth to partisan
choice in the eighteenth century is difficult to ascertain. Data on the
subject are extremely limited for most states. During the provincial
period the available figures show no fundamental difference in the
selection pattern by rich and poor. Candidates received roughly the
same proportion of votes from all segments of society. As Robert
E. and B. Katherine Brown asserted after examining numerous poll
lists in Virginia, "Men at every level tended to scatter their votes instead of voting with any apparent degree of class solidarity."[31]
Similar statements could be made about pre-Revolutionary New
York and Rhode Island.

In the Confederation era, however, the situation may have
changed, and a man's economic background may have guided his
preferences more closely. One contemporary claimed that the election between James Bowdoin and John Hancock in 1787 followed
fairly strict class lines, at least in Boston. Bowdoin, he said, obtained the majority of the ballots from the better sort—gentlemen,
lawyers, doctors, merchants—while Hancock received his support
primarily from the less affluent—laborers, servants, etc. A few
days after the contest, his assessment of the tally among the "different classes of citizens" appeared in the *Massachusetts Centinel*
as shown below.[32]

	For Mr. B	For Mr. H
Physicians	19	2
Clergymen	2	0
Lawyers	17	3
Independent Gentlemen	50	0
Merchants and Traders	295	21
Printers	8	4
Tradesmen	328	299
Labourers, Servants, Etc.	5	446
	724	775

Three days later, a spokesman from the Hancock camp dismissed this arrangement, insisting that Bowdoin's backers were chiefly usurers, speculators, and bank stockholders, while Hancock's votes came from the merchant class and other "worthy members of society."[33] His breakdown is as follows:

	For Mr. B	For Mr. H
Usurers	28	0
Speculators in Public Securities	576	0
Stockholders & Directors of the M——tts B——k	81	0
Persons under British influence	17	0
Merchants, Tradesmen, and other worthy members of society	21	448
Friends to the Revolution	0	327
Wizards	1	0
	724	775

Although these one-sided estimates in Boston may not validate the connection between wealth and partisan choice, a recent examination of Virginia voters in this period by Norman Risjord demonstrates a strong correlation at times existed. Where office seekers could not be distinguished by party or political issue, he says, the electors failed to align themselves on any economic basis. But in those cases in the late 1780s where a full-fledged party contest developed, a significant number of individuals did pursue their own economic interest. The poorest classes generally selected men identified with debtor views and Antifederalism, the middling sort divided evenly, while the wealthy displayed a distinct preference for creditor-oriented Federalism.[34]

The statistics Risjord compiled from four Virginia polls in early 1789 clearly bear out his thesis. Two-thirds of the Federalist vote in two Greensville County elections came from planters owning £150 or more in real property, whereas 72 percent of the Antifederalist vote came from persons with less than £150. An Isle of Wight election that year shows half of the vote received by the Antifederalist candidate was given by non-slaveholders, though only a quarter of the Federalist standard-bearer's tally was drawn from that group. In Amherst County, in the famous congressional contest between James Madison and James Monroe, those possessing few slaves and little property cast more ballots for Monroe than Madison obtained altogether (129 to 110). Madison's backers tended to be wealthier than the county norm in almost every category. On the whole, poor men were twice as likely to support Monroe; rich men were twice as likely to favor Madison.[35]

Yet Risjord's theory of partisan division based on personal wealth cannot be carried too far. While the correlations may be valid for the evidence he has looked at, other results at the time contradict his conclusions. If economic self-interest was the crucial determinant, how can one explain Madison's overall victory against Monroe? Although the vote in Amherst County closely followed class lines, it could not have done so in other parts of the district, such as Culpeper County, where Madison won by 256 to 103, or Orange County, where the tally was 216 to 9. Furthermore, how does one explain the fact that Federalists won seven of the ten congressional seats in Virginia and the vast majority elsewhere? The connection with wealth is equally difficult to establish in the vote a year earlier for members of the state ratifying conventions. In certain places the Federalists won almost unanimously, so that they undoubtedly received backing from poor men as well as from the rich. Thus, even when party division prevailed, voting according to one's economic level was far from universal. Other factors, such as the candidate's personality and achievements, residence, and family ties, were obviously at work too.[36]

In some areas, one of the chief determinants of partisan choice was the people's religious and ethnic background. Many candidates, including James Madison, made appeals to electors on an ethnic or religious basis, hoping that the members of a particular group would all vote the same way. Contemporaries frequently mentioned the "German vote," the "Quaker vote," the "Presbyterian vote," or the "Baptist vote," in reference to an impending election. In 1787-88, at the time of the state ratifying conventions, members of the Baptist church in the northern states, seeking religious equality, apparently voted as a bloc in support of the Federalists, who favored a constitutional amendment guaranteeing freedom of worship. Several newspapers around the nation carried the following item: "We hear that the Baptist Societies in general, in the eastern, as well as the middle States, are much in favor of the new Federal Constitution."[37]

The ethnic-religious dimension of voting is best documented in the states of Pennsylvania and Delaware. In the former, a study of voting behavior in Chester and York counties in 1778–79 by Owen S. Ireland indicates a strong correlation between religious affiliation and partisan choice. The districts in each county which were primarily Presbyterian gave overwhelming support to candidates with similar Calvinist backgrounds. At the same time, the districts which were heavily Anglican, German Lutheran, and Quaker usually backed non-Calvinist office seekers. Moreover, results from the first congressional election in Pennsylvania (1788) shows that German candidates Peter Muhlenberg and Daniel Hiester ran well ahead of other men on the Antifederal ticket in the counties of Philadelphia, Berks, and Northampton, where large numbers of Germans resided. Delaware turnout cannot be subjected to such exact analysis. Yet throughout the period voters in predominantly Scotch-Irish Presbyterian New Castle County generally selected persons of the same orientation, while inhabitants of Sussex County, who were largely Anglican, almost always chose individuals of that persuasion.[38]

However, in New York, where the population was widely mixed, religion and nationality seem to have had relatively little to do with determining political allegiances. As Alfred F. Young has convincingly demonstrated in the election of delegates to that state's ratifying convention in 1788, "there was no clear-cut line-up of any of the major national groups." Despite strong appeals to the electorate on the basis of nationality—Dutch, German, Scottish, etc.—no evidence of partisan alignment among any of them can be found. Some areas dominated by one of these peoples voted one way, some voted the other way. The absence of ethnic influence in the results can also be seen in the fact that New York City, inhabited by many minority elements, was almost completely Federalist, whereas Orange County, with a similar makeup, was almost completely Antifederalist.[39]

All in all, it seems impossible to advance any single theory of voting behavior for the Revolutionary era. While some voted out of a sense of duty or attended for social reasons, most voters came out because they thought they would have an impact. There were many factors influencing the size of the turnout: the restrictiveness of the suffrage qualifications, the types of officials to be selected, the proximity of the bulk of voters to the polls, the age and location of the community, the degree of political maturity and factionalism present, and the relative importance of the issues. A person's inclination to vote was also affected by certain personal characteristics, such as his overall attitude toward government, his ethnic or religious ties, and especially his economic status. It was demonstrated in a number of instances that the greater one's affluence, the greater was the likelihood of one's being an active voter. In regard to partisan choice it is even more difficult to show cause and effect. Yet it is evident that in many cases a man's position on issues, his membership in a faction, and his geographic location were major determinants at the polls. A sharp division was demonstrated between coastal commercial areas and inland agricultural regions in many states. In Pennsylvania and Delaware ethnic and religious attachments were obviously significant. In Virginia, and probably elsewhere, a fairly strong connection existed between wealth and the type of person designated. Those with a good deal of property tended to support Cosmopolitan (Federalist) candidates; those with a lesser amount backed Localist (Antifederalist) types. Perhaps as more data become available they will reveal with greater clarity why men voted the way they did.

Epilogue

From looking at the voting process in the Revolutionary era, it is clear that the American election system had begun to take on many modern, democratic characteristics. The ideology of the Revolution had stressed the belief in government by the people and the framers of the new constitutions and voting laws helped put this into practice. Increased numbers of elected officials, lower suffrage provisions, more equal representation, regular and frequent contests, wider use of paper ballots, and easier access to the polls all became hallmarks of the new system. In addition, fairly stable factions eventually developed in most states, leading to more competitive, issue-oriented politics and heated races for public office. Within this framework other innovations occurred. New types of candidates appeared, nominations became more broadly based, and electioneering expanded. Turnout on election day climbed higher than in the provincial period. In all phases, popular participation was greater than ever before. To be sure, all the changes did not take hold everywhere and many traditional elements would remain part of the picture for a long time to come. However, in the majority of cases new forms were gradually replacing the old. Thus, when the Federalists and Jeffersonians initiated nation-wide campaign efforts in the 1790s, they had much experience, many established institutions, and an active electorate to draw upon. The seeds of the new modern-style election system had already been planted and had started to grow.

Notes

CHAPTER 1

1. Robert J. Dinkin, *Voting in Provincial America: A Study of Elections in the Thirteen Colonies, 1689-1776* (Westport, Conn., 1977).

2. Jackson T. Main, *Political Parties Before the Constitution* (Chapel Hill, 1973), pp. 15-17. See also chap. 6 below.

3. Gordon S. Wood, *The Creation of the American Republic, 1776-1787* (Chapel Hill, 1969); Henry S. Commager, *The Empire of Reason: How Europe Imagined and America Realized the Enlightenment* (Garden City, N.Y., 1977), esp. chap. 7.

4. Wood, *Creation of the American Republic,* esp. chaps. 4-5; Merrill Jensen, "The American People and the American Revolution," *Journal of American History* 57 (June 1970): 5-35; Gouverneur Morris to John Penn, May 20, 1774, in Peter Force, comp., *American Archives* (Washington, 1837-53), 4th ser., 1:343; Jack P. Greene, "Paine, America, and the 'Modernization' of Political Consciousness," *Political Science Quarterly* 93 (Spring 1978): 73-92.

5. The influence of the war in raising political consciousness is stressed in John Shy, *A People Numerous and Armed* (New York, 1976), chap. 9. The quote is in a letter from John Eliot to Jeremy Belknap, January 12, 1777, in Massachusetts Historical Society, *Collections,* 6th ser. iv (1891): 99.

6. John Eliot to Jeremy Belknap, May 9, 1777, in Belknap Papers, Massachusetts Historical Society, Boston.

7. Johann David Schoepf, *Travels in the Confederation* (Philadelphia, 1911), p. 349.

8. Elizabeth Cometti, ed., *Seeing America and Its Great Men: The Journal and Letters of Count Francesco dal Verme, 1783-1784* (Charlottesville, Va., 1969), p. 36.

9. For instructing representatives, see Wood, *Creation of the American Republic,* pp. 188-96, 363-72. The quotation from Samuel Chase is in ibid., p. 371.

10. For an excellent discussion of the impact of issues on elections in the various states, see Main, *Political Parties*. The quotation is taken from Edmund Randolph to James Madison, April 4, 1787, in William T. Hutchinson et al., eds., *The Papers of James Madison* (Chicago, 1962-), 9:364-65.

11. Main, *Political Parties,* esp. chap. 2.

12. Edmund Randolph to James Madison, February 7, 1783, in Hutchinson et al., *Madison Papers,* 6:207.

13. For the Sullivan-Langdon feud, see Charles P. Whittemore, *A General of the Revolution, John Sullivan of New Hampshire* (New York, 1961), chaps. 13-14.

14. Archibald Stuart to Thomas Jefferson, October 17, 1785, in Julian P. Boyd, ed., *The Papers of Thomas Jefferson* (Princeton, 1950-), 8:645.

15. For the best discussion of the special elections in the late 1780s, see Merrill Jensen, ed., *The Documentary History of the Ratification of the Constitution* (Madison, 1976-), and Merrill Jensen and Robert A. Becker, eds., *The Documentary History of the First Federal Elections, 1788-1790* (Madison, 1976-).

16. Kenneth Coleman, *The American Revolution in Georgia* (Athens, Ga., 1958), chaps. 5, 9.

17. Ibid., pp. 193-94. See also William W. Abbot, "The Structure of Politics in Georgia, 1782-1789," *William and Mary Quarterly,* 3d ser. 14 (January 1957): 47-65.

18. Coleman, *Georgia,* chap. 17.

19. For South Carolina politics in this era, see Main, *Political Parties,* chap. 9. See also Richard Walsh, ed., *The Writings of Christopher Gadsden* (Columbia, S.C., 1966), pp. 22-23.

20. For the election of 1784, see Richard Walsh, *Charleston's Sons of Liberty: A Study of the Artisans, 1763-1789* (Columbia, S.C., 1959), pp. 111-23; *South Carolina Gazette,* November 20, 1784.

21. John Lloyd to T.B. Smith, December 7, 1784, quoted in U. B. Phillips, "The South Carolina Federalists," *American Historical Review* 14 (April 1909): 537.

22. The ratification and congressional contests are discussed in George C. Rogers, Jr., *Evolution of a Federalist: William Loughton Smith of Charleston, 1758-1812* (Columbia, S.C., 1962).

23. Robert L. Ganyard, "Radicals and Conservatives in Revolutionary North Carolina: A Point at Issue, the October Election, 1776," *William and Mary Quarterly,* 3d ser. 24 (October 1967): 568-87. The quotation from Nash is in Hugh T. Lefler and Albert R. Newsome, *The History of a Southern State: North Carolina,* 3d ed. (Chapel Hill, 1973), p. 230.

24. For the development of parties in North Carolina, see Norman K. Risjord, *Chesapeake Politics, 1781-1800* (New York, 1978), pp. 72, 88-95. See also Main, *Political Parties,* pp. 311-17.

25. Several contests in these years are vividly described in Griffith J. McRee, *Life and Correspondence of James Iredell* (New York, 1857-58).

26. McRee, *Iredell,* 2:170; Risjord, *Chesapeake Politics,* pp. 317-19.

27. Louise I. Trenholme, *The Ratification of the Federal Constitution in North Carolina* (New York, 1932), p. 107.

28. Risjord, *Chesapeake Politics,* pp. 317–19, 337–41.

29. John Page to Richard Henry Lee, May 6, 1778, quoted in Robert E. and B. Katherine Brown, *Virginia, 1705-1786: Democracy or Aristocracy?* (East Lansing, 1964), p. 289. For Virginia politics in general, see Main, *Political Parties,* chap. 9.

30. Edmund Pendleton to James Madison, March 31, 1783, in Hutchinson et al., *Madison Papers,* 6:423.

31. Edmund Pendleton to James Madison, April 14, 1783, in ibid., 6:461.

32. Risjord, *Chesapeake Politics,* pp. 148–56, 174–79, 203–10.

33. Ibid, pp. 300–306, 326–30.

34. For Maryland politics, see Ronald Hoffman, *A Spirit of Dissension: Economics, Politics, and the Revolution in Maryland* (Baltimore, 1973); and Main, *Political Parties,* chap. 8.

35. L. Marx Renzulli, Jr., *Maryland: The Federalist Years* (Rutherford, N.J., 1972), chaps. 1–2.

36. Ibid., chaps. 2–3; Dorothy M. Brown, "Politics of Crisis: The Maryland Elections of 1788-1789," *Maryland Historical Magazine* 57 (September 1962): 195–209.

37. A detailed account of Pennsylvania politics appears in Robert L. Brunhouse, *The Counter-Revolution in Pennsylvania, 1776-1790* (Harrisburg, 1942). See also Main, *Political Parties,* chap. 7.

38. Brunhouse, *Counter-Revolution,* chaps. 6–7.

39. Delaware politics is treated in Harold B. Hancock, *The Loyalists of Revolutionary Delaware* (Newark, Del., 1977), esp. pp. 55–57, 75. See also John A. Munroe, *Federalist Delaware, 1775-1815* (New Brunswick, N.J., 1954); and Timoleon [pseud.], *The Biographical History of Dionysius, Tyrant of Delaware* (Wilmington, Del., 1788).

40. Hancock, *Loyalists,* pp. 98–100; Munroe, *Federalist Delaware,* pp. 102–8.

41. The authoritative account of New Jersey politics in this era is Richard P. McCormick, *Experiment in Independence: New Jersey in the Critical Period, 1781-1789* (New Brunswick, N.J., 1950), esp. chap. 4. See also Main, *Political Parties,* chap. 6.

42. McCormick, *Experiment in Independence,* chaps. 10–11.

43. The best study of New York politics is found in Alfred F. Young, *The Democratic-Republicans of New York: The Origins, 1763-1797* (Chapel Hill, 1967), chaps. 1–4. See also Main, *Political Parties,* chap. 5.

44. Henry Livingston to Walter Livingston, April 24, 1785, quoted in Main, *Political Parties,* p. 152.

45. The struggle over the Constitution is described in Young, *Democratic-Republicans,* chaps. 4–5; and Linda G. DePauw, *The Eleventh Pillar: New York State and the Federal Constitution* (Ithaca, 1966). The quote is found in Alexander Hamilton to Gouverneur Morris, May 19, 1788, in

Harold C. Syrett et al., eds., *The Papers of Alexander Hamilton* (New York, 1961–79), 4:651.

46. Young, *Democratic-Republicans,* chap. 5.

47. Massachusetts elections are thoroughly analyzed in Van Beck Hall, *Politics Without Parties: Massachusetts, 1780–1791* (Pittsburgh, 1972), esp. chap. 3. See also Main, *Political Parties,* chap. 4.

48. Hall, *Politics Without Parties,* pp. 136–38, 197–99.

49. Ibid., pp. 235–47, 299–304.

50. Ibid., pp. 305–16; Jensen and Becker, *First Federal Elections,* 1:431–742.

51. Connecticut contests are discussed in Philip H. Jordan, "Connecticut Politics During the Revolution and Confederation" (Ph.D. diss., Yale University, 1962), pp. 109–10, 118–19, 130–31.

52. Ibid., pp. 215–18, 255–58, 280–82, 320–31, 371–72.

53. New Hampshire political life is fully described in Jere R. Daniell, *Experiment in Republicanism: New Hampshire Politics and the American Revolution, 1741–1794* (Cambridge, Mass., 1970), chaps. 5–8.

54. Ibid., pp. 192–96; Whittemore, *Sullivan,* pp. 192–216.

55. Whittemore, *Sullivan,* pp. 221–22.

56. Rhode Island politics during the war years is chronicled in Joel A. Cohen, "Rhode Island and the American Revolution: A Selective Socio-Economic Analysis" (Ph.D. diss., University of Connecticut, 1967), pp. 119–21.

57. Ibid., pp. 129, 151.

58. The contests of the late 1780s are dealt with in Irwin H. Polishook, *Rhode Island and the Union, 1774–1795* (Evanston, Ill., 1969), pp. 124–26, 152–54, 198–99; and Main, *Political Parties,* pp. 303–5.

CHAPTER 2

1. For the franchise before independence, see Chilton Williamson, *American Suffrage from Property to Democracy, 1760–1860* (Princeton, 1960), chaps. 1–2; and Robert J. Dinkin, *Voting in Provincial America: A Study of Elections in the Thirteen Colonies, 1689–1776* (Westport, Conn., 1977), chap. 2.

2. Dinkin, *Voting,* pp. 31–32, 36–37.

3. Williamson, *American Suffrage,* p. 76.

4. Joseph Priestley, *An Essay on the First Principles of Government* (London, 1768), p. 41.

5. James Burgh, *Political Disquisitions* (London, 1774–1775), 1:37–38.

6. H. Trevor Colbourn, *The Lamp of Experience: Whig History and the Intellectual Origins of the American Revolution* (Chapel Hill, 1965); Williamson, *American Suffrage,* chap. 4.

7. James Otis, "Considerations on Behalf of the Colonists," *Boston Gazette,* July 22, 1765.

8. A. H. Smyth, ed., *The Writings of Benjamin Franklin* (New York: 1905–7), 10:130–31.

9. Remonstrance of Salem County Freemen, February, 1776, in Richard P. McCormick, *The History of Voting in New Jersey, 1664-1911* (New Brunswick, N.J., 1953), p. 67.

10. Essex [pseud.], "To the Author of Common Sense," February 26, 1776, in Peter Force, comp., *American Archives* (Washington, 1837-53), 4th ser., 4:1498. See also Petition from New Brunswick, in ibid., p. 1504.

11. Edmund Pendleton to Thomas Jefferson, August 10, 1776, in Julian P. Boyd, ed., *The Papers of Thomas Jefferson* (Princeton, 1950-), 1:489. See also Gordon S. Wood, *The Creation of the American Republic, 1776-1787* (Chapel Hill, 1969), pp. 168-69.

12. John Adams to John Sullivan, May 26, 1776, in Charles F. Adams, ed., *The Works of John Adams* (Boston, 1850-56), 9:376.

13. Petition of the Privates of the Military Association of the City and Liberties of Philadelphia, February, 1776, in Samuel Hazard et al., eds., *Pennsylvania Archives* (Philadelphia and Harrisburg, 1852-1935), 8th ser., 8:7406. See also Force, *American Archives,* 4th ser., 6:953; Williamson, *American Suffrage,* pp. 81-82.

14. Williamson, *American Suffrage,* pp. 84, 86-88; *Pennsylvania Packet,* March 18, April 29, 1776.

15. Ronald Hoffman, *A Spirit of Dissension: Economics, Politics and the Revolution in Maryland* (Baltimore, 1973), pp. 169-71.

16. The new suffrage provisions are found in Francis N. Thorpe, ed., *The Federal and State Constitutions, Colonial Charters, and Other Organic Laws* (Washington, 1909). See also "An Address of the Convention," in Oscar and Mary Handlin, eds., *The Popular Sources of Political Authority* (Cambridge, 1966), p. 437.

17. J. Paul Selsam, *The Pennsylvania Constitution of 1776* (Philadelphia, 1936), pp. 138, 188-89; Williamson, *American Suffrage,* pp. 92-96.

18. Elisha P. Douglass, *Rebels and Democrats: The Struggle for Equal Political Rights and Majority Rule During the American Revolution* (Chapel Hill, 1955), chap. 8; Williamson, *American Suffrage,* pp. 110-11.

19. Kenneth Coleman, *The American Revolution in Georgia* (Athens, Ga., 1958), chaps. 4-5; Williamson, *American Suffrage,* pp. 104-5.

20. Richard F. Upton, *Revolutionary New Hampshire* (Hanover, N.H., 1936), chap. 13; Williamson, *American Suffrage,* pp. 105-6.

21. McCormick, *History of Voting,* chap. 3.

22. Hoffman, *Spirit of Dissension,* pp. 180-83; Williamson, *American Suffrage,* pp. 108-10.

23. Bernard Mason, *The Road to Independence: The Revolutionary Movement in New York, 1773-1777* (Lexington, Ky., 1966), pp. 238-42; Williamson, *American Suffrage,* pp. 107-8.

24. J. R. Pole, *Political Representation in England and the Origins of the American Republic* (London, 1966), pp. 172-214; Williamson, *American Suffrage,* pp. 101-3; Handlin, *Popular Sources,* pp. 437, 520.

25. Williamson, *American Suffrage,* p. 111.

26. Edmund Randolph, *History of Virginia,* ed. Arthur H. Shaffer (Charlottesville, Va., 1970), p. 256; Pole, *Political Representation,* pp. 281-96.

27. William W. Hening, ed., *The Statutes at Large . . . of Virginia* (Richmond, 1809-23), 12:120-21.

28. Williamson, *American Suffrage,* p. 112.

29. Ibid., p. 112.

30. Ibid., p. 113.

31. Jackson T. Main, *The Sovereign States, 1775-1783* (New York, 1973), p. 200, claims that overall the increase in the number of new voters was small.

32. The estimate of the number of voters is in the *Pennsylvania Packet,* December 18, 1787.

33. Williamson, *American Suffrage,* pp. 30-31; *New Hampshire Mercury,* March 15, 1785.

34. Williamson, *American Suffrage,* p. 29; McCormick, *History of Voting,* p. 77.

35. Williamson, *American Suffrage,* p. 35.

36. For example, almost half of the adult males turned out in New Castle County in 1785. See results in *Pennsylvania Packet,* October 6, 1785.

37. Robert E. Brown, *Middle-Class Democracy and the Revolution in Massachusetts, 1691-1780* (Ithaca, 1955), chap. 2; Robert J. Taylor, *Western Massachusetts in the Revolution* (Providence, 1954), p. 207; George Minot, *History of the Insurrections in Massachusetts* (Worcester, 1788), pp. 23-24.

38. Williamson, *American Suffrage,* p. 35; J. R. Pole, "Suffrage and Representation in Maryland from 1776 to 1810: A Statistical Note and Some Reflections," *Journal of Southern History* 24 (May 1958): 218-25. Thornton Anderson, "Eighteenth-Century Suffrage: The Case of Maryland," *Maryland Historical Magazine* 76 (June 1981): 149.

39. Charles S. Sydnor, *Gentlemen Freeholders: Political Practices in Washington's Virginia* (Chapel Hill, 1952), p. 142; Jackson T. Main, "Sections and Politics in Virginia, 1781-1787," *William and Mary Quarterly,* 3d ser. 12 (January 1955): 96-112; Robert E. and B. Katherine Brown, *Virginia, 1705-1786: Democracy or Aristocracy?* (East Lansing, 1964), chap. 7.

40. Alfred F. Young, *The Democratic-Republicans of New York: The Origins, 1763-1797* (Chapel Hill, 1967), chap. 4 and appendix.

41. Joel A. Cohen, "Democracy in Rhode Island: A Statistical Analysis," *Rhode Island History* 29 (1970): 5; *Newport Herald,* April 10, 1788.

42. Philip H. Jordan, "Connecticut Politics during the Revolution and Confederation" (Ph.D. diss., Yale University, 1962), pp. 50-51.

43. Charles S. Grant, *Democracy in the Connecticut Frontier Town of Kent* (New York, 1961), pp. 111-12.

44. Kenneth A. Lockridge, "Land, Population and the Evolution of New England Society, 1630-1790," *Past and Present* 39 (April 1968): 62-80.

45. Max Farrand, ed., *The Records of the Federal Convention of 1787* (New Haven, 1937), 2:201.

46. Ibid., pp. 201, 202-3.

47. Ibid., pp. 204–5, 208.
48. For the removal of religious qualifications, see Anson P. Stokes and Leo Pfeffer, *Church and State in the United States,* rev. ed. (New York, 1964), chap. 3; and Sanford H. Cobb, *The Rise of Religious Liberty in America* (New York, 1902), chap. 9.
49. For the voting rights of blacks, see Charles H. Wesley, "Negro Suffrage in the Period of Constitution-Making, 1787–1865," *Journal of Negro History* 32 (April 1947): 143–69; John Hope Franklin, *From Slavery to Freedom,* 4th ed. (New York, 1974), p. 169.
50. Quoted in George H. Moore, *Notes on the History of Slavery in Massachusetts* (New York, 1886), p. 186.
51. Ibid., p. 197. The quotation is taken from Jeremy Belknap to Ebenezer Hazard, January 25, 1788, in Massachusetts Historical Society, *Collections,* 5th ser. iii (1877): 12.
52. Mary Philbrook, "Women's Suffrage in New Jersey," New Jersey Historical Society, *Proceedings* 57 (1939): 87–98.
53. [Theophilus Parsons], *Results of the Convention of Delegates Holden at Ipswich in the County of Essex* (Newburyport, Mass., 1778), p. 29.
54. These statements are based on the new constitutional provisions, which are printed in Thorpe, *Federal and State Constitutions.*
55. For a discussion of the test laws and the postwar treatment of Loyalists, see Merrill Jensen, *The New Nation: A History of the United States during the Confederation, 1781–1789* (New York, 1950), pp. 265–81. The laws are summarized in Claude H. Van Tyne, *The Loyalists in the American Revolution* (New York, 1902), appendix B.

CHAPTER 3

1. Robert J. Dinkin, *Voting in Provincial America: A Study of Elections in the Thirteen Colonies, 1689–1776* (Westport, Conn., 1977), chap. 3.
2. Elisha P. Douglass, *Rebels and Democrats: The Struggle for Equal Political Rights and Majority Rule During the American Revolution* (Chapel Hill, 1955), pp. 116, 333–34.
3. *The People the Best Governors; or, A Plan of Government Founded on the Just Principles of Natural Freedom* (n.p., 1776), p. 9; "Democritus," *Massachusetts Spy* (Worcester), July 5, 1775.
4. *Massachusetts Spy* (Worcester), July 12, 26, 1775; The Watchman [pseud.], *To the Inhabitants of the City and County of New York* (New York, 1776).
5. Marquis de Chastellux, *Travels in North America,* ed. Howard Rice (Chapel Hill, 1963), 1:162.
6. The new property qualifications are compiled from the various state constitutions in Francis N. Thorpe, ed., *The Federal and State Constitutions, Colonial Charters, and Other Organic Laws* (Washington, 1909). See also Willi P. Adams, *The First State Constitutions* (Chapel Hill, 1980); and

Thornton Anderson, "Maryland's Property Qualifications for Office: A Reinterpretation of the Constitutional Convention of 1776," *Maryland Historical Magazine* 73 (December 1978), 327-39.

7. David Ramsay, "An Oration on the Advantages of American Independence, spoken before a Public Assembly of the Inhabitants of Charleston, in South Carolina, on July 4th, 1778," in Hezekiah Niles, ed., *Principles and Acts of the Revolution in America* (Baltimore, 1822; reprint ed., New York, 1971), p. 65.

8. For the changes in religious qualifications, see Anson P. Stokes and Leo Pfeffer, *Church and State in the United States,* rev. ed. (New York, 1964), chap. 3; and Sanford H. Cobb, *The Rise of Religious Liberty in America* (New York, 1902), chap. 9.

9. "The Memorial of Rabbi Gershom Seixas" (December 23, 1783), in Morris U. Schappes, ed., *A Documentary History of the Jews in the United States, 1654-1875,* 3d ed. (New York, 1971), p. 65.

10. Age requirements are taken from the constitutions in Thorpe, *Federal and State Constitutions.*

11. Pennsylvania Constitution, sec. 7, Maryland Constitution, sec. 15, New York Constitution, sec. 17, Massachusetts Constitution, Declaration of Rights, Art. 18, in ibid., 3:1694, 1892, 5:2632, 3084.

12. Residence requirements are taken from the constitutions in ibid. See also Gordon S. Wood, *The Creation of the American Republic, 1776-1787* (Chapel Hill, 1969), pp. 181-88.

13. Richard Henry Lee to Edmund Pendleton, May 12, 1776, in James C. Ballagh, ed., *The Letters of Richard Henry Lee* (New York, 1911-14), 1:191.

14. Pennsylvania Constitution, sec. 8, South Carolina Constitution, sec. 28, in Thorpe, *Federal and State Constitutions,* 5:3084, 6:3254; Wood, *Creation of the American Republic,* pp. 140-41.

15. Wood, *Creation of the American Republic,* pp. 150-59.

16. "Rationalis," Broadside (Philadelphia, 1776). See also *To the Several Battalions of Military Associators in the Province of Pennsylvania* (Philadelphia, 1776); *Pennsylvania Packet,* November 26, 1776, February 6, 1779.

17. *Massachusetts Centinel,* August 23, 1788. See also *New Jersey Gazette,* October 10, 1785.

18. *New York Packet,* April 14, 1785. See also ibid., April 7, 1785; *Independent Gazetteer* (Philadelphia), October 11, 1783.

19. *New York Daily Advertiser,* April 5, 1786.

20. Cumberland County, New Jersey, Committee, August 7, 1776, in Peter Force, comp., *American Archives* (Washington, 1837-53), 5th ser., 1:812.

21. Columbus [pseud.], "To the Electors of the City and County of New York," June 12, 1776, in ibid., 4th ser., 6:825-26. See also *Providence Gazette,* April 10, 17, 1779.

22. *New Hampshire Spy,* December 12, 1788. See also *New Hampshire Gazette,* March 11, 1786; *Worcester Magazine,* November 1787, p. 112.

23. "Plato's Letters, No. 1," *United States Chronicle* (Providence),

April 12, 1787; *Providence Gazette,* April 7, 1787.
24. *To the Voters of Baltimore* (Baltimore, September 25, 1787).
25. James Warren to John Adams, May 18, 1787, in *The Warren-Adams Letters,* Massachusetts Historical Society, *Collections* (1925), 73:293. See also Thomas Sumter to Charles Pinckney, January 27, 1789, in Merrill Jensen and Robert A. Becker, eds., *The Documentary History of the First Federal Elections, 1788-1790* (Madison, 1976-), 1:210.
26. James Madison to Edmund Randolph, February 11, 1783, and Randolph to Madison, March 22, 1783, in William T. Hutchinson et al., eds., *The Papers of James Madison* (Chicago, 1962-), 6:223, 380; George Mason to Martin Cockburn, April 18, 1784, in Robert A. Rutland, ed., *The Papers of George Mason, 1725-1792* (Chapel Hill, 1970), 2:799-800.
27. Turnover is based on figures in Norman K. Risjord and Gordon DenBoer, "The Evolution of Political Parties in Virginia, 1782-1800," *Journal of American History* 60 (March 1974): 962; *New Jersey Gazette,* 1787-88; John R. Bartlett, ed., *Records of the Colony of Rhode Island and Providence Plantations* (Providence, 1856-65).
28. Samuel Johnston to Mrs. James Iredell, May 15, 1784, in Griffith J. McRee, *Life and Correspondence of James Iredell* (New York, 1857-58), 2:100-101.
29. Jackson T. Main, "Government by the People: The American Revolution and the Democratization of the Legislatures," *William and Mary Quarterly,* 3d ser. 23 (July 1966): 393-97.
30. Ibid., p. 404.
31. Ibid., pp. 399-406.
32. Roger Atkinson to Samuel Pleasants, November 23, 1776, in *Virginia Magazine of History and Biography* 15 (1908): 357.
33. *Gazette of the State of Georgia* (Savannah), January 1, 1789.
34. Wayne L. Bockelman and Owen S. Ireland, "The Internal Revolution in Pennsylvania: An Ethnic-Religious Interpretation," *Pennsylvania History* 41 (April 1974): 125-59; Benjamin Franklin to William Strahan, August 19, 1784, quoted in Owen S. Ireland, "The Ethnic-Religious Dimension of Pennsylvania Politics, 1778-1779," *William and Mary Quarterly,* 3d ser. 30 (July 1973): 424-25.
35. Robert L. Brunhouse, *The Counter-Revolution in Pennsylvania, 1776-1790* (Harrisburg, 1942), pp. 2-3.
36. Joel A. Cohen, "Democracy in Rhode Island: A Statistical Analysis," *Rhode Island History* 29 (1970): 6-7.
37. Edward M. Cook, Jr., *The Fathers of the Towns: Leadership and Community Structure in Eighteenth-Century New England* (Baltimore, 1976), pp. 185-92.
38. Ibid., p. 192.

CHAPTER 4

1. For nominations prior to independence, see Robert J. Dinkin, *Voting in Provincial America: A Study of Elections in the Thirteen Colo-*

nies, 1689-1776 (Westport, Conn., 1977), chap. 4.

2. David Humphreys to John Humphreys, August 4, 1786, in Frank L. Humphreys, *Life and Times of David Humphreys* (New York, 1917), 1:359.

3. *New Jersey Gazette,* August 21, 1782.

4. *Virginia Independent Chronicle,* January 7, 1789.

5. Ibid., January 14, 1789.

6. For criticism of public nominations, see *Connecticut Courant,* September 9, 1783; and *Hampshire Gazette,* December 17, 1788. The quotation is taken from Joseph Barrell to Boston Town Committee, June 4, 1778, in Worthington C. Ford, ed., *Correspondence and Journals of Samuel Blachley Webb* (New York, 1893; reprint ed., 1969), 2:101.

7. William Hooper to James Iredell, April 8, 1782, in Griffith J. McRee, *Life and Correspondence of James Iredell* (New York, 1857-58), 2:11.

8. William Hill to Thomas Person, April 24, 1780, in Walter Clark, ed., *The State Records of North Carolina* (Winston and Goldsboro, 1886-1914), 14:803.

9. Donald Jackson and Dorothy Twohig, eds., *The Diaries of George Washington* (Charlottesville, Va., 1976-), 4:312.

10. Lawrence Taliaferro to James Madison, December 16, 1787, in Gaillard Hunt, ed., *The Writings of James Madison* (New York, 1900-1910), 5:71. See also Archibald Maclaine to James Iredell, December 25, 1787, in McRee, *Iredell,* 2:183.

11. *Virginia Independent Chronicle,* March 21, 28, 1787.

12. Richard A. Ryerson, *The Revolution is Now Begun: The Radical Committees of Philadelphia, 1765-1776* (Philadelphia, 1978); Charles S. Olton, *Artisans for Independence: Philadelphia Mechanics and the American Revolution* (Syracuse, 1975), pp. 87, 93; Staughton Lynd, *Class Conflict, Slavery, and the United States Constitution* (Indianapolis and New York, 1967), pp. 100-108.

13. For county conventions in general, see Robert J. Taylor, *Western Massachusetts in the Revolution* (Providence, 1954), esp. chaps. 5-7. The quotation appears in *Massachusetts Spy* (Worcester), March 25, 1784.

14. *Pennsylvania Journal,* September 3, 1777; Robert L. Brunhouse, *The Counter-Revolution in Pennsylvania, 1776-1790* (Harrisburg, 1942), p. 9.

15. *At a Meeting of Deputies of Kent County* (Dover, Del., 1783).

16. A nomination meeting in the Southwark district of Philadelphia in 1783 was attended by 159 persons; see *Independent Gazetteer* (Philadelphia), October 11, 1783.

17. *New Jersey Gazette,* September 4, 1782. See also *New Jersey Journal,* September 24, 1788; and various issues of the *Pennsylvania Packet* for early October, beginning in 1785.

18. Richard P. McCormick, *Experiment in Independence: New Jersey in the Critical Period, 1781-1789* (New Brunswick, N.J., 1950), pp. 76-77; *Carlisle Gazette,* October 4, 1786.

19. Robert J. Dinkin, "The Nomination of Governor and Assistants in Colonial Connecticut," *Connecticut Historical Society Bulletin* 36 (July 1971): 92–96.

20. "A True Republican," *Connecticut Courant,* September 9, 1783.

21. "To the Discontent People of America," ibid.

22. *Norwich Packet,* April 8, 1784.

23. George Washington to David Stuart, December 2, 1788, in John C. Fitzpatrick, ed., *The Writings of George Washington* (Washington, 1930–44), 30:147. See also Washington to Henry Lee, December 12, 1788, in ibid., p. 156.

24. Henry Lee to James Madison, December 8, 1788, in William T. Hutchinson et al., eds., *The Papers of James Madison* (Chicago, 1962–), 11:388.

25. *Maryland Journal,* December 26, 1788.

26. Ibid., December 28, 1788.

27. *United States Chronicle* (Providence), February 16, 1786; Irwin H. Polishook, *Rhode Island and the Union, 1774–1795* (Evanston, Ill., 1969), pp. 42–43.

28. Samuel Ward to Welcome Arnold, April 7, 1786, Manuscript Collections, Rhode Island Historical Society, Providence.

29. *Providence Gazette,* April 11, 1789.

30. Neil Andrews, Jr., "The Development of the Nominating Convention in Rhode Island," Rhode Island Historical Society, *Proceedings* 1 (1892–93): 258–69.

31. *American Herald* (Boston), March 27, 1786; *Massachusetts Centinel,* March 29, 1786.

32. *American Herald* (Boston), March 27, 1786.

33. *Massachusetts Centinel,* May 6, 1786.

34. Ibid., February 14, 1787; *Independent Chronicle* (Boston), February 15, March 15, 1787.

35. *Worcester Magazine,* March 1787, pp. 637–39.

36. The different tickets are in *Massachusetts Centinel,* November 28, December 1, 5, 1787; *American Herald* (Boston), December 3, 1787; *Independent Chronicle* (Boston), December 6, 1787; *Boston Gazette,* December 3, 1787. Christopher Gore to Rufus King, December 9, 1787, in Charles R. King, ed., *The Life and Correspondence of Rufus King* (New York, 1894–1900), 1:262.

37. *Massachusetts Centinel,* December 8, 1787.

38. Steven R. Boyd, *The Politics of Opposition* (Millwood, N.Y., 1979), p. 87; *Massachusetts Centinel,* March 29, 1788.

39. Jackson T. Main, *Political Parties Before the Constitution* (Chapel Hill, 1973), pp. 150–53; Lynd, *Class Conflict,* pp. 100–108.

40. Main, *Political Parties,* pp. 151–52; *New York Journal,* April 22, 1784; *Independent New York Gazette,* December 20, 27, 1783; *New York Packet,* March 31, April 4, 7, 14, 18, 21, 25, 1785.

41. Main, *Political Parties,* pp. 152–53; *New York Gazetteer, and the Country Journal,* April 20, 27, 1786.

42. Linda G. DePauw, *The Eleventh Pillar: New York State and the Federal Constitution* (Ithaca, 1966), pp. 123-30.

43. Alfred F. Young, *The Democratic-Republicans of New York: The Origins, 1763-1797* (Chapel Hill, 1967), pp. 130-32; *New York Daily Advertiser,* February 21, 1789.

44. *Pennsylvania Packet,* September 30, 1785, September 29, 1786; John Simpson to James Potter, September 27, 1788, in Merrill Jensen and Robert A. Becker, eds., *The Documentary History of the First Federal Elections, 1788-1790* (Madison, 1976-), 1:290.

45. *Pennsylvania Packet,* October 3, 6, 7, 1785, September 29, 1786.

46. Ibid., October 6, 10, 1787; *Independent Gazetteer* (Philadelphia), October 9, 1787.

47. Boyd, *Politics of Opposition,* pp. 52-53; *Carlisle Gazette,* October 24, 31, 1787.

48. *Independent Gazetteer* (Philadelphia), November 1, 6, 1787.

49. Material relating to Antifederalist nominations for the first federal Congress is in Jensen and Becker, *First Federal Elections,* 1:229-81. The quotation is taken from the Cumberland Circular Letter in ibid., p. 240.

50. The Antifederal ticket was first printed in the *Federal Gazette* (Philadelphia), November 7, 1788.

51. Ibid., October 15, 1788; *Pennsylvania Packet,* October 17, 20, 27, 1788.

52. See items related to the Lancaster Convention in Jensen and Becker, *First Federal Elections,* 1:313-31. The original ticket was published in the *Pennsylvania Packet,* November 10, 1788.

53. The movement to add Germans to both tickets is documented in Jensen and Becker, *First Federal Elections,* 1:339-64. See especially "To the German Inhabitants of the State of Pennsylvania," in ibid., pp. 339-40.

CHAPTER 5

1. See Robert J. Dinkin, *Voting in Provincial America: A Study of Elections in the Thirteen Colonies, 1689-1776* (Westport, Conn., 1977), chaps. 1, 5.

2. Edmund Randolph to James Madison, March 22, 1783, in William T. Hutchinson et al., eds., *The Papers of James Madison* (Chicago, 1962-), 6:380.

3. Griffith J. McRee, *Life and Correspondence of James Iredell* (New York, 1857-58), 2:170-71.

4. J. R. Pole, *Political Representation in England and the Origins of the American Republic* (London, 1966), p. 237; Charles S. Sydnor, *Gentlemen Freeholders: Political Practices in Washington's Virginia* (Chapel Hill, 1952), pp. 42-46; David Thomas to Griffith Evans, March 3, 1789, in Massachusetts Historical Society, *Proceedings* 46 (1913): 371; John Sullivan to John Wendell, March 14, 1785, in Otis G. Hammond, ed., *The Letters and Papers of Major-General John Sullivan,* New Hampshire Historical Society, *Collections* (1939), 15:411.

5. William Hooper to James Iredell, July 6, 1785, in McRee, *Iredell,* 2:125. See also Iredell to Pierce Butler, March 14, 1784, in ibid., p. 93.

6. James Madison to George Washington, December 2, 1788, in Hutchinson et al., *Madison Papers,* 11:377.

7. Quoted in E. Wilder Spaulding, *His Excellency George Clinton* (New York, 1938), p. 189. Electioneering for the March gubernatorial race in New Hampshire can be seen in early February newspapers, for example, *New Hampshire Mercury,* February 1, 1785; *New Hampshire Gazette,* February 4, 1785.

8. Jasper Yeates to James Burd, October 10, 1778, in Thomas Balch, ed., *Letters and Papers Relating Chiefly to the Provincial History of Pennsylvania* (Philadelphia, 1855), p. 267.

9. Letter to John Stevens, Sr., October 1, 1784, quoted in Richard P. McCormick, *Experiment in Independence: New Jersey in the Critical Period, 1781-1789* (New Brunswick, N.J., 1950), pp. 78-79.

10. Robert McClallen to James Duane, March 12, 1788, quoted in Clarence E. Miner, *The Ratification of the Federal Constitution by the State of New York* (New York, 1921), p. 87. See also Burgess Ball to James Madison, December 8, 1788, in Hutchinson et al., *Madison Papers,* 11:385-86.

11. Miner, *Ratification,* p. 94; Robert Livingston to James Duane, April 30, 1788, and Thomas Tillotson to Robert R. Livingston, March 23, 1787, in Alfred F. Young, *The Democratic-Republicans of New York: The Origins, 1763-1797* (Chapel Hill, 1967), pp. 95, 96.

12. Dorothy M. Brown, "Politics of Crisis: The Maryland Elections of 1788-89," *Maryland Historical Magazine* 57 (September 1962): 203; *Pennsylvania Evening Herald,* October 12, 1785, October 4, 1786.

13. Quoted in Robert A. Rutland, *The Ordeal of the Constitution* (Norman, Okla., 1966), pp. 206-7.

14. *Pennsylvania Evening Herald,* October 12, 1785.

15. "Extracts from the Letter-Books of Lieutenant Enos Reeves of the Pennsylvania Line," in *Pennsylvania Magazine of History and Biography* 21 (1897): 385-86.

16. Hugh Williamson to John G. Blount, August 21, 1785, in Alice B. Keith and William H. Masterson, eds., *The John Gray Blount Papers* (Raleigh, 1952-65), 1:207; Archibald Maclaine to William Hooper, March 12, 1783, in Walter Clark, ed., *The State Records of North Carolina* (Winston and Goldsboro, 1886-1914), 16:945; Maclaine to James Iredell, August 3, 1786, in McRee, *Iredell,* 2:144.

17. Anthony Wayne to John Hannum, January 9, 1786, quoted in Jackson T. Main, *Political Parties Before the Constitution* (Chapel Hill, 1973), p. 205.

18. Timoleon [pseud.], *The Biographical History of Dionysius, Tyrant of Delaware* (Wilmington, 1788), pp. 43-44; *Massachusetts Centinel,* March 14, 1789.

19. Philip Schuyler to John Jay, May 30, 1785, in Henry P. Johnston, ed., *The Correspondence and Public Papers of John Jay* (New York, 1890-93), 3:151-52.

20. Herbert S. Allan, *John Hancock, Patriot in Purple* (New York,

1948), p. 266; Alexander Hamilton to Robert Morris, August 13, 1782, in Harold C. Syrett et al., eds., *The Papers of Alexander Hamilton* (New York, 1961–79), 3:137–38.

21. William Plumer to John Sullivan, March 14, 1787, in Colonial Society of Massachusetts, *Publications* 11 (1907): 402.

22. Christopher Gore to Rufus King, March 2, 1788, in Charles R. King, ed., *The Life and Correspondence of Rufus King* (New York, 1894–1900), 1:323.

23. Rutland, *Ordeal of the Constitution,* pp. 37–38, 117–18, 128, 138, 169, 199, 209.

24. Linda G. DePauw, *The Eleventh Pillar: New York State and the Federal Constitution* (Ithaca, 1966), pp. 125–26, 138; L. Marx Renzulli, *Maryland: The Federalist Years* (Rutherford, N.J., 1972), pp. 53, 75, 75n.

25. Van Beck Hall, *Politics Without Parties: Massachusetts, 1780–1791* (Pittsburgh, 1972), pp. 274–75; Irving Brant, *James Madison* (Indianapolis, 1941–61), 3:241–42.

26. For a general discussion of treating, see Sydnor, *Gentlemen Free-holders,* pp. 51–59. Treating seems to have expanded in New England; see David Syrett, "Town-Meeting Politics in Massachusetts, 1776–1786," *William and Mary Quarterly,* 3d ser. 21 (July 1964): 364; *Independent Chronicle* (Boston), April 2, 1789. The quotation is taken from J. Thomas Scharf, *History of Maryland* (Baltimore, 1879), 2:548n.

27. Edmund Pendleton to Richard Henry Lee, March 14, 1785, in David J. Mays, ed., *The Letters and Papers of Edmund Pendleton* (Charlottesville, Va., 1967), 2:477. See also Pendleton to James Madison, April 9, 1789, in ibid., 2:556.

28. Young, *Democratic-Republicans,* p. 96.

29. Abraham Yates, "Speeches to Delegates in Congress, 1786," quoted in Staughton Lynd, *Class Conflict, Slavery, and the United States Constitution* (Indianapolis and New York, 1967), p. 39.

30. DePauw, *Eleventh Pillar,* p. 133; *Massachusetts Centinel,* March 30, 1785; *Independent Chronicle* (Boston), March 31, 1785.

31. Henry Jackson to Henry Knox, January 11, 1789, in Merrill Jensen and Robert A. Becker, eds., *The Documentary History of the First Federal Elections, 1788–1790* (Madison, 1976–), 1:644.

32. Elmer C. Griffith, *The Rise and Development of the Gerrymander* (Chicago, 1907), pp. 31–43; Brant, *Madison,* 3:237–40.

33. For the expansion of newspapers in the Revolutionary era, see Alfred M. Lee, *The Daily Newspaper in America* (Lawrence, Kan., 1937), chaps. 1–3; and Sidney Kobre, *The Development of American Journalism* (Dubuque, Ia., 1969), chap. 3.

34. Hall, *Politics Without Parties,* p. 84.

35. *Massachusetts Centinel,* April 2, 1785.

36. Tench Coxe to Robert Smith, August 5, 1788, in Jensen and Becker, *First Federal Elections,* 1:248. See also Albany Anti-Federal Committee to the New York Committee, April 12, 1788, quoted in Young, *Democratic-Republicans,* p. 88.

37. *To the Worthy and Industrious Mechanicks of the State* (New York, 1783); *To the Whig Mechanicks of the City and County of New York* (New York, 1783); *To the Electors of the City of New York* (New York, 1783); *To the Worthy Inhabitants of Baltimore Town* (Baltimore, 1786); *To the Voters of Anne Arundel County* (Annapolis, 1786).

38. Robert L. Brunhouse, *The Counter-Revolution in Pennsylvania, 1776-1790* (Harrisburg, 1942), p. 3; Brown, "Politics of Crisis," p. 198; Timoleon [pseud.], *Dionysius*, pp. 58-59. The quotation is taken from Rudolph J. and Margaret C. Pasler, *The New Jersey Federalists* (Cranbury, N.J., 1975), p. 29.

39. *Pennsylvania Packet,* November 26, 1776; *To the Several Battalions of Military Associators in the Province of Pennsylvania* (Philadelphia, 1776).

40. *New York Packet,* April 14, 1785.

41. *Maryland Journal,* September 5, 1788. In addition, see Renzulli, *Maryland,* pp. 40, 61, 72, 108.

42. Renzulli, *Maryland,* chaps. 1-3; Brown, "Politics of Crisis."

43. *Independent Gazetteer* (Philadelphia), October 7, 1786.

44. *New Hampshire Gazette,* February 4, 1785.

45. *Massachusetts Spy* (Worcester), June 2, 1785.

46. David Thomas to Griffith Evans, March 3, 1789, in Massachusetts Historical Society, *Proceedings* 46 (1913): 371.

47. Jonathan Jackson to Oliver Wendell, January 11, 1789, in Jensen and Becker, *First Federal Elections,* 1:628.

CHAPTER 6

1. For a full discussion of voting procedures in the years before 1776, see Robert J. Dinkin, *Voting in Provincial America: A Study of Elections in the Thirteen Colonies, 1689-1776* (Westport, Conn., 1977), chap. 6.

2. The movement to establish short-term elections is described in Gordon S. Wood, *The Creation of the American Republic, 1776-1787* (Chapel Hill, 1969), pp. 165-67. The quotation is taken from "The Interest of America" (1776), in Peter Force, comp., *American Archives* (Washington, 1837-53), 4th ser., 6:840-843.

3. [Carter Braxton], "Address to the Convention of the Colony and Ancient Dominion of Virginia" (1776), in Force, *American Archives,* 4th ser., 6:748-753; Thomas Jefferson to Samuel Adams, February 26, 1800, in William V. Wells, *The Life and Public Services of Samuel Adams* (Boston, 1865), 3:368; Wood, *Creation of the American Republic,* pp. 166-67.

4. The provisions for officeholders are found in the various state constitutions in Francis N. Thorpe, ed., *The Federal and State Constitutions, Colonial Charters, and Other Organic Laws* (Washington, 1909).

5. For the specific dates of election, see the state constitutions in ibid.

6. The numbers of representatives are derived from the published and unpublished state legislative journals.

7. *South Carolina and American General Gazette* (Charleston), December 31, 1778.

8. The attempt to expand and equalize representation is discussed in Wood, *Creation of the American Republic,* chap. 5; J. R. Pole, *Political Representation in England and the Origins of the American Republic* (London, 1966), pp. 172–204; Lester J. Cappon et al., eds., *Atlas of Early American History: The Revolutionary Era, 1760–1790* (Princeton, 1976), pp. 131–32.

9. The new provisions are summarized in Cappon et al., *Atlas,* pp. 131–32.

10. Ibid., p. 132; Pole, *Political Representation,* pp. 172–204.

11. Cappon et al., *Atlas,* p. 132.

12. See provisions in Thorpe, *Federal and State Constitutions.*

13. The regulations concerning the conduct of elections are found either in the state constitutions or in separate election statutes. See, for example, the Pennsylvania election law of 1777 in James T. Mitchell and Henry Flanders, eds., *The Statutes at Large of Pennsylvania from 1682 to 1809* (Harrisburg, 1896–1911), 9:114–23.

14. Nathaniel Bouton et al., eds., *Documents and Records Relating to New Hampshire* (Concord and Manchester, 1867–1941), 11:44–45, 355, 422, 465, 703.

15. David Syrett, "Town-Meeting Politics in Massachusetts, 1776–1786," *William and Mary Quarterly,* 3d ser. 21 (July 1964): 357–58.

16. Walter Clark, ed., *State Records of North Carolina* (Winston and Goldsboro, 1886–1914), 12:69; *Laws of the State of New York, 1777–1801* (Albany, 1886–87), sess. 1, chap. 16 (1778); *Pennsylvania Statutes at Large,* 12:25; Syrett, "Town-Meeting Politics," p. 356.

17. *State Gazette of South Carolina,* November 10, 1788.

18. *Laws of New York,* sess. 1, chap. 16 (1778); Alfred F. Young, *The Democratic-Republicans of New York: The Origins, 1763–1797* (Chapel Hill, 1967), p. 87n.

19. Richard P. McCormick, *The History of Voting in New Jersey, 1664–1911* (New Brunswick, N.J., 1953), pp. 73–81.

20. *Pennsylvania Statutes at Large,* 9:116–20, 12:25–52.

21. For changes in the election sites in New Jersey, see *New Jersey Archives* (Newark, 1880–1906), 2d ser., 3:416; for Pennsylvania, see *Pennsylvania Statutes at Large,* 9:116–20.

22. See the various state constitutions in Thorpe, *Federal and State Constitutions.* For the New Jersey congressional election of 1789, see Richard P. McCormick, *Experiment in Independence: New Jersey in the Critical Period, 1781–1789* (New Brunswick, N.J., 1950), pp. 296–99.

23. *New Hampshire Gazette,* March 4, 1789; *Laws of New York,* sess. 1, chap. 16 (1778); Allen D. Candler, ed., *The Colonial Records of the State of Georgia* (Atlanta, 1904–16), 19:361; *Pennsylvania Statutes at Large,* 12:25–52, 290–96; Robert L. Brunhouse, *The Counter-Revolution in Pennsylvania, 1776–1790* (Harrisburg, 1942), pp. 6–7.

24. Plymouth Town Records, March 25, 1776, quoted in Syrett,

"Town-Meeting Politics," p. 355.

25. Merrill Jensen and Robert A. Becker, eds., *The Documentary History of the First Federal Elections, 1788-1790* (Madison, 1976-), 1:369, 370, 374.

26. Fitch E. Oliver, ed., *The Diary of William Pynchon of Salem* (Boston and New York, 1890), p. 77. See also ibid., pp. 96, 124.

27. *State Gazette of South Carolina,* April 10, 1788.

28. Hugh Williamson to John Gray Blount, August 21, 1785, in Alice B. Keith and William H. Masterson, eds., *The John Gray Blount Papers* (Raleigh, 1952-65), 1:208.

29. Samuel B. Webb to Miss Hogeboom, April 27, 1788, Webb to Joseph Barrell, May 11, 1788, in Worthington C. Ford, ed., *Correspondence and Journals of Samuel Blachley Webb* (New York, 1893; reprint ed., 1969), 3:98, 102.

30. Brunhouse, *Counter-Revolution,* p. 8; Harold B. Hancock, *The Delaware Loyalists* (Wilmington, Del., 1940), p. 42; McCormick, *Experiment in Independence,* p. 92; *New Jersey Journal* (Elizabeth), October 29, 1788.

31. McCormick, *Experiment in Independence,* p. 82.

32. William W. Hening, ed., *The Statutes at Large . . . of Virginia* (Richmond, 1809-23), 12:127.

33. *Laws of New York,* sess. 1, chap. 16 (1778).

34. Charles S. Sydnor, *Gentlemen Freeholders: Political Practices in Washington's Virginia* (Chapel Hill, 1952), chap. 2.

35. *To the Freeholders . . .* (New York, 1770); *The People the Best Governors* (n.p., 1776), p. 13; Force, *American Archives,* 4th ser., 6:731.

36. See the New York Constitution in Thorpe, *Federal and State Constitutions,* 5:2630 (Article VI).

37. McCormick, *History of Voting,* pp. 65-66, 73-76, 79-80.

38. *Pennsylvania Statutes at Large,* 9:115.

39. Syrett, "Town-Meeting Politics," p. 362.

40. Michael Zuckerman, *Peaceable Kingdoms: New England Towns in the Eighteenth Century* (New York, 1970), pp. 183-84; Syrett, "Town-Meeting Politics," pp. 362-65.

41. Candler, *Georgia Records,* 19:361; Clark, *North Carolina Records,* 12:69; *Pennsylvania Statutes at Large,* 9:115; McCormick, *Experiment in Independence,* pp. 87-88.

42. Clark, *North Carolina Records,* 12:69; *Laws of New York,* sess. 1, chap. 16 (1778); *Pennsylvania Statutes at Large,* 9:122.

43. Brunhouse, *Counter-Revolution,* pp. 8-9; Keith and Masterson, *Blount Papers,* 1:528-29; Syrett, "Town-Meeting Politics," p. 363.

44. For disputed elections, see Clark, *North Carolina Records,* 12:557, 21:122; Theodora J. Thompson, ed., *South Carolina: Journals of the House of Representatives, 1783-1784* (Columbia, S.C., 1977), p. 283; *Archives of Maryland,* 71:60-61.

45. Jensen and Becker, *First Federal Elections,* 1:543, 770.

46. Hening, *Statutes,* 12:127.

CHAPTER 7

1. Voter turnout is based on the state figures given below. Percentages are determined from population statistics in Evarts B. Greene and Virginia D. Harrington, *American Population Before the Federal Census of 1790* (New York, 1932); and W. S. Rossiter, *A Century of Population Growth, 1790–1900* (Washington, 1909). As several states present census data for males with age sixteen as determining manhood, one-fifth of the number given has been subtracted in order to account for those men between the ages of sixteen and twenty-one.

2. Data for the period prior to independence are taken from Robert J. Dinkin, *Voting in Provincial America: A Study of Elections in the Thirteen Colonies, 1689–1776* (Westport, Conn., 1977), chap. 7. For comparative figures after 1789, see J. R. Pole, *Political Representation in England and the Origins of the American Republic* (London, 1966), pp. 544–45, 554–56.

3. New Hampshire gubernatorial returns for 1784 are derived from the town meeting records in the Microfilm Collection, New Hampshire State Library, Concord. The results from 1785 to 1789 are in Nathaniel Bouton et al., eds., *Documents and Records Relating to New Hampshire* (Concord and Manchester, 1867–1941), 20:306, 580, 21:9–10, 263, 587. Figures for presidential Electors and congressmen are in ibid., 21:258–59, 433, 437.

4. Most of the Rhode Island statistics have been provided by Professor Edward M. Cook, University of Chicago. The full gubernatorial vote for 1787 appeared in the *United States Chronicle* (Providence), May 10, 1787, while the referendum on the Constitution is recorded in Rhode Island, General Assembly Reports, 1778–1788, p. 122, Rhode Island State Archives, Providence.

5. The estimated Pennsylvania totals are derived from data in Samuel Hazard et al., eds., *Pennsylvania Archives* (Philadelphia and Harrisburg, 1852–1935), 6th ser.: 11, and Robert L. Brunhouse, *The Counter-Revolution in Pennsylvania, 1776–1790* (Harrisburg, 1942), appendix 2.

6. The voting figures for Maryland sheriff races are taken from Election Returns, Box 1, 1776–1789, Maryland Hall of Records, Annapolis. Other results are found in *Pennsylvania Packet,* October 16, 1786; *Maryland Journal* (Baltimore), October 5, 1787, April 11, 15, May 16, 1788; *Maryland Gazette,* January 22, 1789.

7. Massachusetts gubernatorial results are in Abstracts of Votes for Governor and Lieutenant-Governor, Massachusetts Archives, Boston. Figures for the first federal elections are in Merrill Jensen and Robert A. Becker, eds., *The Documentary History of the First Federal Elections, 1788–1790* (Madison, 1976–), 1:609–23.

8. Sources for the Connecticut gubernatorial elections are the following: 1780 and 1784: Franklin B. Dexter, ed., *The Literary Diary of Ezra Stiles* (New York, 1901), 2:423, 3:120; 1781–83: Jonathan Trumbull, Sr., Diary; 1780–85: Jonathan Trumbull Papers, 9:39, 59, 64, Connecticut Historical Society, Hartford; 1786: Civil Officers, 2d ser., 5:233c, Connecticut Archives, Hartford; 1787: Jedediah Huntington to Andrew Huntington, May 1787, in Connecticut Historical Society, *Collections* (1923),

20:471; 1788: *New Haven Gazette,* May 15, 1788. The ratification figures are from Merrill Jensen, ed., *The Documentary History of the Ratification of the Constitution* (Madison, 1976-), 3:411, 414, 417, 431.

9. Alfred F. Young, *The Democratic-Republicans of New York: The Origins, 1763-1797* (Chapel Hill, 1967), p. 86.

10. New York gubernatorial results are in ibid., pp. 24, 29, 34, 143; data pertaining to the ratification contests are on pp. 89-90. New York City assembly results are from *Independent New York Gazette,* January 3, 1784; *New York Packet,* May 2, 1785, May 1, 1786.

11. New Jersey returns are as follows: Hunterdon: 1782, 1784, 1785: *New Jersey Gazette,* October 23, 1782, October 25, 1784, October 24, 1785; Burlington: 1783, Poll List, AM Papers, New Jersey State Library, Trenton; 1787, *Pennsylvania Magazine of History and Biography* 44 (1920): 77-81; Essex: 1785, *Political Intelligencer* (New Brunswick), October 26, 1785; 1788, *New York Daily Advertiser,* October 21, 1788; Sussex: 1785, *New Jersey Gazette,* October 31, 1785; Monmouth: 1785, ibid., December 12, 1785. The congressional returns (1789) are in *Pennsylvania Packet,* March 24, 1789.

12. Delaware figures for 1776 are located in *Minutes of the Council of the Delaware State from 1776 to 1792* (Wilmington, 1887), p. 9. The other returns are in *Pennsylvania Packet,* October 6, 1785; *Maryland Journal,* January 20, 1789; *Pennsylvania Mercury,* October 10, 1789.

13. See report on "A Bill Concerning the Election of Members of General Assembly," in Julian P. Boyd, ed., *The Papers of Thomas Jefferson* (Princeton, 1950-), 3:346.

14. Virginia returns are taken primarily from Robert E. and B. Katherine Brown, *Virginia, 1705-1786: Democracy or Aristocracy?* (East Lansing, 1964), p. 289; Charles S. Sydnor, *Gentlemen Freeholders: Political Practices in Washington's Virginia* (Chapel Hill, 1952), pp. 137-40; Norman K. Risjord, "How the 'Common Man' Voted in Jefferson's Virginia," in John B. Boles, ed., *America: The Middle Period, Essays in Honor of Bernard Mayo* (Charlottesville, Va., 1973), pp. 36-64. There are a few items from newspapers and other sources: *Virginia Independent Chronicle,* March 5, 1788; *Virginia Herald and Fredericksburg Advertiser,* March 27, 1788, February 12, 1789; Gaillard Hunt, ed., *The Writings of James Madison* (New York, 1900-1910), 5:318.

15. The few scattered North Carolina results are found in Walter Clark, ed., *The State Records of North Carolina* (Winston and Goldsboro, 1886-1914), 15:190, 16:945; Alice B. Keith and William H. Masterson, eds., *The John Gray Blount Papers* (Raleigh, 1952-57), 1:208, 340; Griffith J. McRee, *The Life and Correspondence of James Iredell* (New York, 1857-58), 2:11, 94; Louise I. Trenholme, *The Ratification of the Federal Constitution in North Carolina* (New York, 1932), p. 12.

16. For South Carolina, the St. Andrew's Parish return is found in Theodora J. Thompson, ed., *South Carolina: Journals of the House of Representatives, 1783-1784* (Columbia, S.C., 1977), p. 283. The Charleston figures are recorded in *Gazette of the State of South Carolina,* September 17, 1783; *South Carolina Gazette and General Advertiser,* September 14,

1784; *South Carolina Historical Magazine* 61 (January 1955): 45-49; *State Gazette of South Carolina,* December 4, 1786, December 4, 1788; *Columbia Herald,* April 17, 1788. Statistics for the congressional race are in Jensen and Becker, *First Federal Elections,* 1:198-99.

17. Allen D. Candler, ed., *The Colonial Records of the State of Georgia* (Atlanta, 1904-16), 3:436.

18. Chatham County (Savannah) results are in *Georgia Gazette,* December 4, 1783, December 9, 1784, December 6, 1787, and December 4, 1788.

19. Figures for the special elections are in Jensen, *Ratification* (Madison, 1976-), and Jensen and Becker, *First Federal Elections.* The estimate by Forrest McDonald is in his *E Pluribus Unum: The Formation of the American Republic, 1776-1790* (Boston, 1965), p. 197.

20. *Maryland Journal* (Baltimore), April 15, 1788.

CHAPTER 8

1. For an attempt to analyze voting behavior in the period before 1776, see Robert J. Dinkin, *Voting in Provincial America: A Study of Elections in the Thirteen Colonies, 1689-1776* (Westport, Conn., 1977), chap. 8.

2. Suffrage restrictions are discussed in chapter 2 above. The comparative figures for the New York election of 1788 are in Alfred F. Young, *The Democratic-Republicans of New York: The Origins, 1763-1797* (Chapel Hill, 1967), p. 85.

3. Voting returns for each state are in chapter 7 above. The gubernatorial vote in New Hampshire was usually 25 to 30 percent higher than the tally for state senators. In 1789, for example, there were about 8,500 ballots cast for governor, 6,400 for senators. Figures are in Nathaniel Bouton et al., eds., *Documents and Records Relating to New Hampshire* (Concord and Manchester, 1867-1941), 21:587, 539.

4. Statistics for the gubernatorial races are in Abstracts of Votes for Governor and Lieutenant-Governor, Massachusetts Archives, Boston; local data are in *Report of the Record Commissioners of the City of Boston* (Boston, 1876-1909), 26:152, 196, 247, 297, 309, 31:2, 24, 69, 98, 114, 135, 148, 161, 171; Franklin P. Rice, ed., *Worcester Town Records* (Worcester, 1879-95), 4:419, 5:27, 39, 69, 111, 137.

5. Richard P. McCormick, *The History of Voting in New Jersey, 1664-1911* (New Brunswick, N.J., 1953), p. 84.

6. See figures in chapter 7 above.

7. Massachusetts statistics are derived from Abstracts of Votes; New Hampshire's are taken from the town meeting records in the Microfilm Collection, New Hampshire State Library, Concord. Montgomery and Columbia county figures are in *New York Journal,* June 5, 1788.

8. See returns for each state in chapter 7.

9. For Massachusetts, see Abstracts of Votes, 1786 and 1787; for Anne Arundel County, Maryland, see Election Returns, Box 1, 1776-1789, Maryland Hall of Records, Annapolis; and *Pennsylvania Packet,* October 16, 1786.

10. Johnston Town Meeting Records, 1754–1791 (Transcripts), Rhode Island Historical Society, Providence.

11. *Federal Gazette* (Philadelphia), October 8, 1788; *Massachusetts Spy,* March 9, 1786. See also Young, *Democratic-Republicans,* pp. 86–87; *Pennsylvania Packet,* February 10, 1789.

12. See figures in Robert L. Brunhouse, *The Counter-Revolution in Pennsylvania, 1776–1790* (Harrisburg, 1942), appendix 2; and Young, *Democratic-Republicans,* pp. 589, 590.

13. Percentages of voters eligible for each office are based on statistics in Young, *Democratic-Republicans,* p. 587.

14. Norman K. Risjord, "How the 'Common Man' Voted in Jefferson's Virginia," in John B. Boles, ed., *America: The Middle Period, Essays in Honor of Bernard Mayo* (Charlottesville, Va., 1973), pp. 36–64.

15. Ibid., p. 63.

16. Dinkin, *Voting,* chap. 8.

17. See Pennsylvania figures in Brunhouse, *Counter-Revolution,* appendix 2; Maryland figures in Philip A. Crowl, *Maryland During and After the Revolution* (Baltimore, 1947), pp. 165–68; New York results are in *New York Packet,* May 30, June 3, 1788; *New York Journal,* June 5, 1788; *New York Daily Advertiser,* June 6, 1788; Rhode Island returns are in *United States Chronicle* (Providence), May 10, 1787.

18. Massachusetts statistics are found in Van Beck Hall, *Politics without Parties, 1780–1791* (Pittsburgh, 1972), pp. 137, 239, 319; Rhode Island figures have been provided by Professor Edward M. Cook, University of Chicago; New Hampshire figures are taken from the town meeting records, Microfilm Collection, New Hampshire State Library.

19. *Independent Gazetteer* (Philadelphia), November 27, 1786.

20. Edmund Randolph to James Madison, April 11, 1787, in William T. Hutchinson et al., eds., *The Papers of James Madison* (Chicago, 1962–), 9:373.

21. John Dawson to James Madison, April 15, 1787, in *Madison Papers,* 9:381–82.

22. *American Herald* (Boston), December 11, 1786.

23. "Agricola," *Pennsylvania Packet,* February 6, 1779.

24. Theodore Sedgwick to Rufus King, June 18, 1787, in Charles R. King, ed., *The Life and Correspondence of Rufus King* (New York, 1894–1900), 1:224.

25. Edmund Randolph to James Madison, March 22, April 11, 1787, in *Madison Papers,* 9:328, 373.

26. John Quincy Adams to John Adams, June 30, 1787, in Worthington C. Ford, ed., *The Writings of John Quincy Adams* (New York, 1913–17), 1:31.

27. Quoted in Herbert S. Allan, *John Hancock, Patriot in Purple* (New York, 1948), p. 266.

28. Mercy Otis Warren to Elbridge Gerry, June 6, 1783, in C. Harvey Gardiner, *A Study in Dissent: The Warren-Gerry Correspondence, 1776–1792* (Carbondale, Ill., 1968), p. 163.

29. Brunhouse, *Counter-Revolution,* p. 8; Nathaniel Whitaker, *The Reward of Toryism* (Newburyport, Mass., 1783), p. 31; "Petition of Cumberland Inhabitants, November 7, 1786," in McCormick, *History of Voting,* p. 80. See also ibid., pp. 82–83.

30. Abraham Yates, "Speeches to Delegates in Congress, 1786," quoted in Staughton Lynd, *Class Conflict, Slavery, and the United States Constitution* (Indianapolis and New York, 1968), p. 39.

31. Robert E. and B. Katherine Brown, *Virginia, 1705–1786: Democracy or Aristocracy?* (East Lansing, 1964), p. 187.

32. *Massachusetts Centinel,* April 4, 1787.

33. Ibid., April 7, 1787.

34. Risjord, "How the 'Common Man' Voted," p. 52.

35. Ibid., pp. 39–46.

36. Risjord admits that even after the formation of national parties in the late 1790s "about a third of the electorate seemed unconcerned with party differences, at least to the extent of supporting two candidates with opposite views." Ibid., p. 64.

37. *Virginia Herald* (Fredericksburg), January 15, 1789; *Worcester Magazine,* October 1787, p. 64. See also *American Mercury* (Hartford), November 5, 1787.

38. Owen S. Ireland, "The Ethnic-Religious Dimension of Pennsylvania Politics, 1778–1779," *William and Mary Quarterly,* 3d ser. 30 (July 1973): 423–48; figures for the first congressional election are in Brunhouse, *Counter-Revolution,* pp. 343–44.

39. Young, *Democratic-Republicans,* pp. 98–99.

Bibliographical Essay

★★★★★★★★★★★★★

To study the subject of voting in the Revolutionary era, one must consult a wide variety of sources. Perhaps most basic are the general collections of printed documents which deal with this period, especially Peter Force, comp., *American Archives,* 9 vols. (Washington, 1837–53); Francis N. Thorpe, ed., *The Federal and State Constitutions, Colonial Charters, and Other Organic Laws,* 7 vols. (Washington, 1909); and two recent works still in progress, Merrill Jensen, ed., *The Documentary History of the Ratification of the Constitution* (Madison, 1976–); and Merrill Jensen and Robert A. Becker, eds., *The Documentary History of the First Federal Elections, 1788–1790* (Madison, 1976–). On the state level, very useful collections include Nathaniel Bouton et al., eds., *Documents and Records Relating to New Hampshire* (Concord and Manchester, 1867–1941); Walter Clark, ed., *State Records of North Carolina,* 30 vols. (Winston and Goldsboro, 1886–1914); and Samuel Hazard et al., eds., *Pennsylvania Archives,* 119 vols. in 9 series (Philadelphia and Harrisburg, 1852–1935). Also valuable are the compilations of state laws such as *Laws of the State of New York, 1777–1801* (Albany, 1886–87); J. T. Mitchell and Henry Flanders, eds., *Statutes at Large of Pennsylvania from 1682 to 1801,* 18 vols. (Harrisburg, 1896–1915); and William H. Hening, ed., *The Statutes at Large of . . . Virginia,* 13 vols. (Richmond, 1809–23).

Newspapers, pamphlets, and broadsides provide another mine of information. Many of the newspapers of the period are now on microfilm or microcards, which are listed in *Newspapers in Microform: United States, 1948–1972* (Washington, 1973). Others, not reproduced, are noted in Clarence S. Brigham, *History and Bibliography of American Newspapers, 1690–1820,* 2 vols. (Worcester, 1947). Pamphlets, broadsides, and periodical literature are indexed in Charles Evans, comp., *American Bibliography: A Chronological Dictionary of All Books, Pamphlets and Periodical Publications . . . 1639 . . . 1820,* 14 vols. (Chicago and Worcester, 1903–59); and Roger P. Bristol, comp., *Supplement to Charles Evans' American*

Bibliography (Charlottesville, Va., 1970); or listed alphabetically in Clifford K. Shipton and James E. Mooney, comps., *National Index of American Imprints Through 1800: The Short-Title Evans,* 2 vols. (Barre, Mass., 1969).

The personal letters and papers of notable figures comprise another major source. Most illuminating on the subject of state politics and elections are William T. Hutchinson et al., eds., *The Papers of James Madison* (Chicago, 1962–); Griffith J. McRee, *Life and Correspondence of James Iredell,* 2 vols. (New York, 1857–58); and *The Warren–Adams Letters,* Massachusetts Historical Society, *Collections* (1917, 1925), vols. 72–73. Also helpful are Julian P. Boyd, ed., *The Papers of Thomas Jefferson,* 19 vols. (Princeton, 1950–); Robert A. Rutland, ed., *The Papers of George Mason, 1725–1792,* 3 vols. (Chapel Hill, 1970); David J. Mays, ed., *The Letters and Papers of Edmund Pendleton,* 2 vols. (Charlottesville, Va., 1967); Harold C. Syrett, ed., *The Papers of Alexander Hamilton,* 26 vols. (New York, 1961–79). Some important collections, such as the Livingston Papers and the James Duane Papers at the New York Historical Society, remain unpublished.

Among general secondary works, some of which deal with several phases of the election process, most significant by far are Jackson T. Main, *Political Parties Before the Constitution* (Chapel Hill, 1973); Gordon S. Wood, *The Creation of the American Republic, 1776–1787* (Chapel Hill, 1969); and J. R. Pole, *Political Representation in England and the Origins of the American Republic* (London, 1966). Pole has also written numerous articles concerning voting in individual states. Other useful studies are Elisha P. Douglass, *Rebels and Democrats: The Struggle for Equal Political Rights and Majority Rule During the American Revolution* (Chapel Hill, 1955); William N. Chambers, *Political Parties in a New Nation: The American Experience, 1776–1809* (New York, 1963); Merrill Jensen, *The New Nation: A History of the United States During the Confederation, 1781–1789* (New York, 1950); and Allan Nevins, *The American States During and After the Revolution, 1775–1789* (New York, 1927). Critical works on the framing and ratification of the United States Constitution, which say a good deal about voting in this era, are Forrest McDonald, *We the People: The Economic Origins of the Constitution* (Chicago, 1958); Robert E. Brown, *Charles Beard and the Constitution* (Princeton, 1956); and Robert A. Rutland, *The Ordeal of the Constitution: The Antifederalists and the Ratification Struggle of 1787–1788* (Norman, Okla., 1966).

On specialized subjects, Chilton Williamson, *American Suffrage from Property to Democracy, 1760–1860* (Princeton, 1960), is vital on the franchise question. Jackson T. Main, "Government by the People: The American Revolution and the Democratization of the Legislatures," *William and Mary Quarterly,* 3d ser. 23 (July 1966): 391–407; idem, *The Upper Houses in Revolutionary America, 1763–1788* (Madison, 1967); James K. Martin,

Men in Rebellion: Higher Governmental Leaders and the Coming of the American Revolution (New Brunswick, N.J., 1973); and Edward M. Cook, Jr., *The Fathers of the Towns: Leadership and Community Structure in Eighteenth-Century New England* (Baltimore, 1976), are all valuable for the changing patterns in officeholding. Although dated, George D. Luetscher, *Early Political Machinery in the United States* (Philadelphia, 1903), is still informative on certain structural developments.

Several state studies are indispensable, including Van Beck Hall, *Politics Without Parties: Massachusetts, 1780–1791* (Pittsburgh, 1972); Jere Daniell, *Experiment in Republicanism: New Hampshire Politics and the American Revolution* (Cambridge, Mass., 1970); Philip H. Jordan, "Connecticut Politics During the Revolution and Confederation" (Ph.D. dissertation, Yale University, 1962); Joel A. Cohen, "Rhode Island and the American Revolution: A Selective Socio-Economic Analysis" (Ph.D. dissertation, University of Connecticut, 1967); Irwin H. Polishook, *Rhode Island and the Union, 1774–1795* (Evanston, Ill., 1969); Alfred F. Young, *The Democratic-Republicans of New York: The Origins, 1763–1797* (Chapel Hill, 1967); Richard P. McCormick, *Experiment in Independence: New Jersey in the Critical Period, 1781–1789* (New Brunswick, N.J., 1950); Robert L. Brunhouse, *The Counter-Revolution in Pennsylvania, 1776–1790* (Harrisburg, 1942); John A. Munroe, *Federalist Delaware, 1775–1815* (New Brunswick, N.J., 1954); Harold B. Hancock, *The Loyalists of Revolutionary Delaware* (Newark, Del., 1977); Ronald Hoffman, *A Spirit of Dissension: Economics, Politics, and the Revolution in Maryland* (Baltimore, 1973); L. Marx Renzulli, Jr., *Maryland: The Federalist Years* (Rutherford, N.J., 1972); Kenneth Coleman, *The American Revolution in Georgia* (Athens, Ga., 1958); Norman K. Risjord, *Chesapeake Politics, 1781–1800* (New York, 1978), an excellent regional study; and finally, Risjord's essay "How the 'Common Man' Voted in Jefferson's Virginia," in John B. Boles, ed., *America: The Middle Period, Essays in Honor of Bernard Mayo* (Charlottesville, Va., 1970).

Index

About the Author

Robert J. Dinkin is Professor of History at California State University in Fresno. *Voting in Revolutionary America* is a sequel to his previous work *Voting in Provincial America* (Greenwood Press, 1977). His articles have appeared in the *New England Quarterly* and the *Historian*.